Finding Success in Vocabulary: The Elementary Years

Grades 3-5

Dr. Candace Jones

© Copyright 2023-Dr. Candace Jones

All rights reserved. This book is protected by the copyright laws of the United States of America. No part of this publication may be reproduced, distributed, stored in a retrieval system, or transmitted in any form or by any means, electronic, mechanical, photocopying, recording or otherwise, without the prior written permission of the copyright holder.

For permission requests, write to the author at the address below.
Dr.Jones@ExpandedEducationalServices.com
Memphis, Tennessee 38141

This book was edited, formatted, designed, and published by:
    UNIQUE PUBLISHING HOUSE, LLC
    P.O. Box 750792, Memphis, TN 38175
    www.uniquehouse.org

ISBN: 979-8-9877059-7-1

Finding Success in Vocabulary: The Elementary Years

Grades 3-5

Dr. Candace Jones

Part One

How to Use this Book

Instructor, please take the time to process through all of part one yourself before introducing it to your students. Once you have it, then you can make sure your students understand it thoroughly before moving into the vocabulary lessons. When working with your students it is essential that you utilize the strategy completely. Do not try to alter or skip parts of it as you may not achieve the desired results if you do.

The EES Success Academy Vocabulary System called Finding Success in Vocabulary: The Middle Years is a unique strategy. It is specially formulated to ensure that each student's vocabulary increases throughout the school year. An increased vocabulary improves reading comprehension, boosts confidence, and enhances verbal communication.

*You will want to remove all the tests and exams from the book before beginning the program.

How to Find Success in Vocabulary

INTRODUCTION TO CRITICAL THINKING

My name is Dr. Candace Jones. I am the founder and Visionaire behind EES Success Academy. In case you do not know, we do things very differently at this school. We prepare students to walk in success in academics and in life.

Vocabulary is an essential part of your personal development. One of the best ways to showcase your level of intelligence is with the level of words that you use. After grade three, it is time to begin replacing lower-level words *(caterpillar words)* with higher level words *(butterfly words)*. If you are older than 10 and still using the same words you used when you were a toddler, that's unacceptable. Your vocabulary must increase with your age. Have no fear though, EES Success Academy's specialized vocabulary system, Finding Success in Vocabulary: Level 2 will have your personal vocabulary up to par in no time.

When attempting to increase your vocabulary, it's necessary to understand how your brain is wired. Here is some food for thought: one word you learned when you were an infant was *good*. Your mom smiled and cooed at you as she told you "good job, you finished your bottle". She also told you, "good job; you went potty all by yourself!" You began using that word as soon as you could talk. When you are describing things now, please be sure to use a synonym more commiserate with your age, yet still means *good*. Perhaps you could use the word *satisfactory* or *delightful* in lieu of *good*. This is but one example of the vocabulary elevation you need to attain.

When it comes to increasing your vocabulary, it is important that you understand how your brain works. Your brain has two types of memory - long term and short term. Information stored in the short-term memory will not be kept. At some point it will be dumped out and forgotten. Whenever you try to cram or quickly memorize information over a short period of time to pass a test, that information will only end up in the short-term memory.

Whenever you purposefully use your new words, every opportunity that you get, by putting them in conversations, putting them in your daily writing assignments, thinking about them, and looking for opportunities to use them on a daily basis, that information will filter over into your long-term memory. Information stored in the long-term memory will be there forever.

It is essential that you make your vocabulary words your very own by ensuring those words get into your long-term memory. At EES-SA, we don't want to give out new words on Monday only to have our students wait until the end of the week to cram the words in the night before the test- happily dumping them onto the test paper earning an A. The problem with this is that after the test, you will NOT remember the words.

There is a way, however, to ensure that your words stay with you forever. When your words stay with you forever, you can easily use them in everyday conversations. Your brain needs processes to retain information. Our process is simple. The EES-SA vocabulary strategy process is that you will be given the definition of each word in short easy to understand phrases. Next, you will use a word web to brainstorm context clues to help you SEE the word meanings. Lastly, you will write meaningful sentences. We will detail this process further in the next section.

Vocabulary & Meaningful Sentences

VOCABULARY: 3 PROCESSES

Since your brain needs processes in order to help it retain information in your long-term memory, we will give it three complete processes to help it retain your new vocabulary words forever. This vocabulary course is to be completed on a week-by-week basis. Your instructor may decide, however, to spend up to two weeks per lesson. Each week on Monday, you will start a new lesson. You will go through all three of the processes each week, being mindful to employ the prescribed strategies throughout the week to ensure these words are getting into your long-term memory. Follow this program and you'll be impressing people with your stellar intellect in no time!

Here is an example of a meaningful sentence written using a new vocabulary word:

malodorous - extremely bad smell
1. *rotten eggs*
2. *dead animal*
3. *skunk scent*

The skunk's spray was malodorous: Its extremely bad odor caused us to gag.

The new word is malodorous. The first thing we should do is notice that the word is made of three parts. I can see that the base word is odor. I know that's a type of smell. I see the prefix is mal. I know *mal* means bad. Finally, the suffix *ous* means *full of*. This is a word I can figure out just by looking at it. Not all new words are like this one.

At any rate, next the definition tells me malodorous means extremely bad odor just like the parts of the word itself tell me it means full of bad odor. Since the suffix tells me this word applies to situations where the smell is fully bad and the definition tells me extremely, I know that this smell is worse than *stinky*. It could even be worse than *funky*, so malodorous is an extreme level of funk. To get a good picture of the word in my mind, I'm going to brainstorm some things that come to mind that are malodorous. Immediately, I visualize rotten eggs, the scent of a dead animal in the hot sun and the spray of a skunk. These images, called context clues, help me see what the new word means so that I can easily internalize the meaning of the new word. Now that I can see it, I can effortlessly insert the new word in my daily writing and in my conversations.

Most textbooks place brand new words in bold print. They use meaningful sentences to help convey the meaning of the word to the reader. It's easier for you, the reader, to use context clues to figure out what the word means than to stop and grab a dictionary. You will use this same practice to ensure that you can always *know* and *see* what your new words mean. Next you will learn to write meaningful sentences.

Meaningful sentences are full of meaning! They contain the new word, one context clue and the definition of the new word. Packing all this learning goodness into one sentence means we will have to use a compound sentence. Compound sentences require the use of a colon. Meaningful sentences work best when they are constructed in this manner: new word + context clue + complete definition.

Process #1: Make a word web that includes the new word in the middle, the definition on the top, and three examples of what the words LOOKS like as context clues. Noteworthy, a context clue can never be *people*. Context clues describe what the people are doing; have done; or what they are known for. For instance, I cannot say *Lisa is malodorous*, because Lisa is *not* a smell. She is a person that has a bad odor. Thus, I will have to say, *Lisa has a malodorous stench; She has an extremely bad smell*.

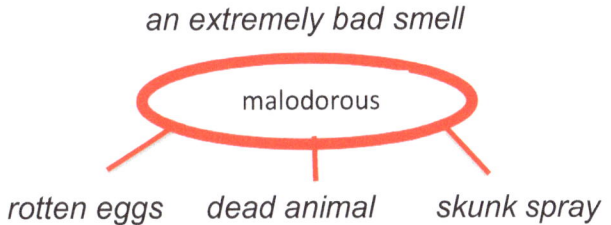

Process #2: Select one context clue and practice using your new word by writing a sentence that is full of meaning. When writing your sentence, always pair the vocabulary word with the context clue. The definition can stand alone. Be sure to include the entire definition. Don't be tempted to shorten it just because it's long. After you have done this to all your words, you will move on to the next phase.

The rotten eggs in the fridge are malodorous; They have an extremely bad smell.

Process #3: Complete a final draft and implement one more process of highlighting your word pink, your context clue yellow, and your definition blue.

I really want you to retain your words. The way this will happen is to ensure that you use processes and intentional daily practice to retain the words. I challenge you to find creative ways to ensure you use and retain your words. I suggest you purposely use your words in conversation in the classroom, around the school, at home and even in your text messages. Our level 2 words are semi-high school level, so chances are your friends and perhaps even some family outside of our school may not understand your words when you use them. Don't let that deter you from using them though. Use them and teach *them* the meanings when they look at you dumbfounded. Don't let them tease you into being ashamed of having a healthy vocabulary though. You challenge them to come up to your level because you will definitely not remain on an old caterpillar level all of your life!

Sometimes students struggle to write a proper meaningful sentence. The objective is to write two complete sentences and connect them with a semicolon. Here is a mistake that I see often, the student will write one complete sentence and one fragment, connecting them both with a semicolon.

lumber – wood sawed into boards; timber

<u>I bought some pine lumber at Home Depot</u>; ~~wood sawed into boards; timber~~

Can you see the problem with this attempt at a meaningful sentence? Yes. It is exactly as I said above. This student wrote one complete sentence (underlined) and one fragment (strikethrough). I chose to strike through the fragment to show the student that that is not a complete sentence. Since part of it is a fragment, the entire thing is wrong, and no credit can be awarded because you have not demonstrated that you understand the process nor that you understand how the semicolon punctuation mark functions. It will have to be redone. Also, it is not necessary to use both parts of the definition in a sentence. One of them will do. Sometimes the definition will have multiple examples included to further increase your understanding of the vocabulary word.

*Instructor, continue practicing with your students and have them use the checklist to police their own work until they completely understand the concepts.

Vocabulary Checklist

 Before you turn in your vocabulary, complete this checklist.

- ❏ DO NOT USE THE INTERNET FOR **ANY** REASON!
- ❏ Use an ink pen.
- ❏ Staple your papers - revision on top, rough draft on the bottom.
- ❏ Head your paper with only your section number, your name and the lesson number.
- ❏ **PAGE ONE** - Do you have a rough draft?
- ❏ Does each word have a completed word web? Word webs include -
    - ❏ Vocabulary word
    - ❏ Definition
    - ❏ 3 context clues
    - ❏ Write a meaningful sentence, but do not highlight it!
- ❏ Did you write 2 complete sentences for each word? [No fragments allowed!]
    - ❏ Do not put the word and the definition in the same sentence!
    - ❏ Did you include the **entire** definition?
    - ❏ Are your context clues examples of the word? Context Clues can **never** be people. Context clues **describe** what the people are doing or have done.
    - ❏ Edit the sentence - remove any lower-level words like "good", "bad" and "very". *for grades 3+
- ❏ **PAGE TWO** - Do you have a revision page?
    - ❏ Number the paper, then write only your sentences.
    - ❏ Highlight the sentences. Highlight ONLY the word, context clue and definition - do not include extra words in your highlighting. PINK - vocabulary YELLOW - context clue BLUE - definition.
- ❏ Is the paper messy? If there are scratch outs and messy writing - redo it.

Parts of Speech and their Usage

When writing your meaningful sentences, you need to understand how to use different parts of speech. You will find that many of your words are adjectives that describe people's characteristics and or behaviors in addition to various situations and circumstances.

Thus, you should never use an adjective as a noun. Likewise, you should never try to use an adjective without a noun. An adjective needs a noun to describe. Resist the urge to write your sentence like this:

cursory (adj) - done hastily without thought for perfection

done hastily without thought for perfection

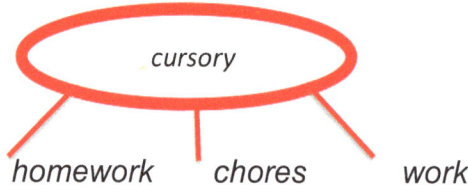

Ana did her homework cursory; It was done hastily without thought for perfection.

Since cursory is an adjective, it describes the way in which Ana did the homework. So, I have to include that information in the sentence after the word. It should say:

Ana did her homework in a cursory manner. It was done hastily without thought for perfection.

~ Enjoy the journey of enhancing your vocabulary this year. You are going to be even more awesome and super intelligent than you already are. I pray this school year is filled with nothing but success for you. Enjoy the journey!

Candace Jones, Ed.D.

Part Two

Lesson 1

1. **impossible** - not able to happen; unreal
2. **fraction** - part of a whole
3. **physician** - a person trained to treat illness; a doctor
4. **enjoyment** - pleasure; satisfaction
5. **avoid** - to stay away from ; to keep out of the way of ; to dodge
6. **nonsense** - foolishness ; silliness ; something that doesn't make sense

L1 MEANINGFUL SENTENCES

Make a word web and write a meaningful sentence for each word in this lesson. Never try to write a meaningful sentence without first creating a word web. The word web is a part of the process for helping you transfer your new knowledge into your long-term memory. This page is your rough draft of the assignment. On a piece of notebook paper, number one-ten and rewrite each meaningful sentence. Highlight the vocabulary word pink, the context clue yellow and the definition blue. You will turn the final draft in for grading.

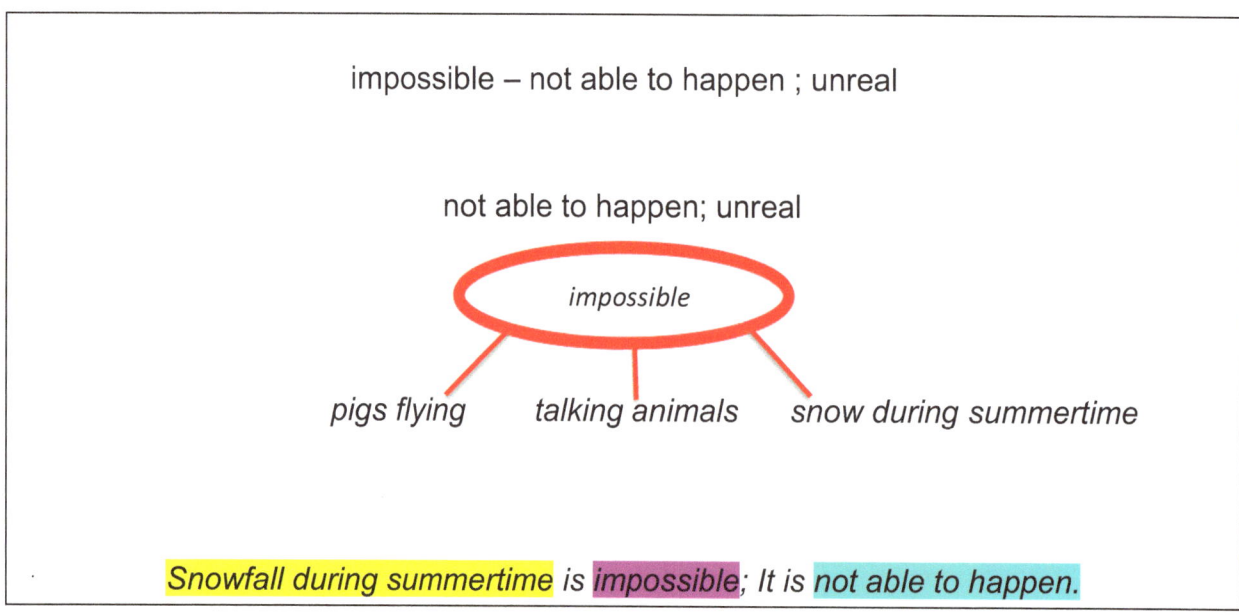

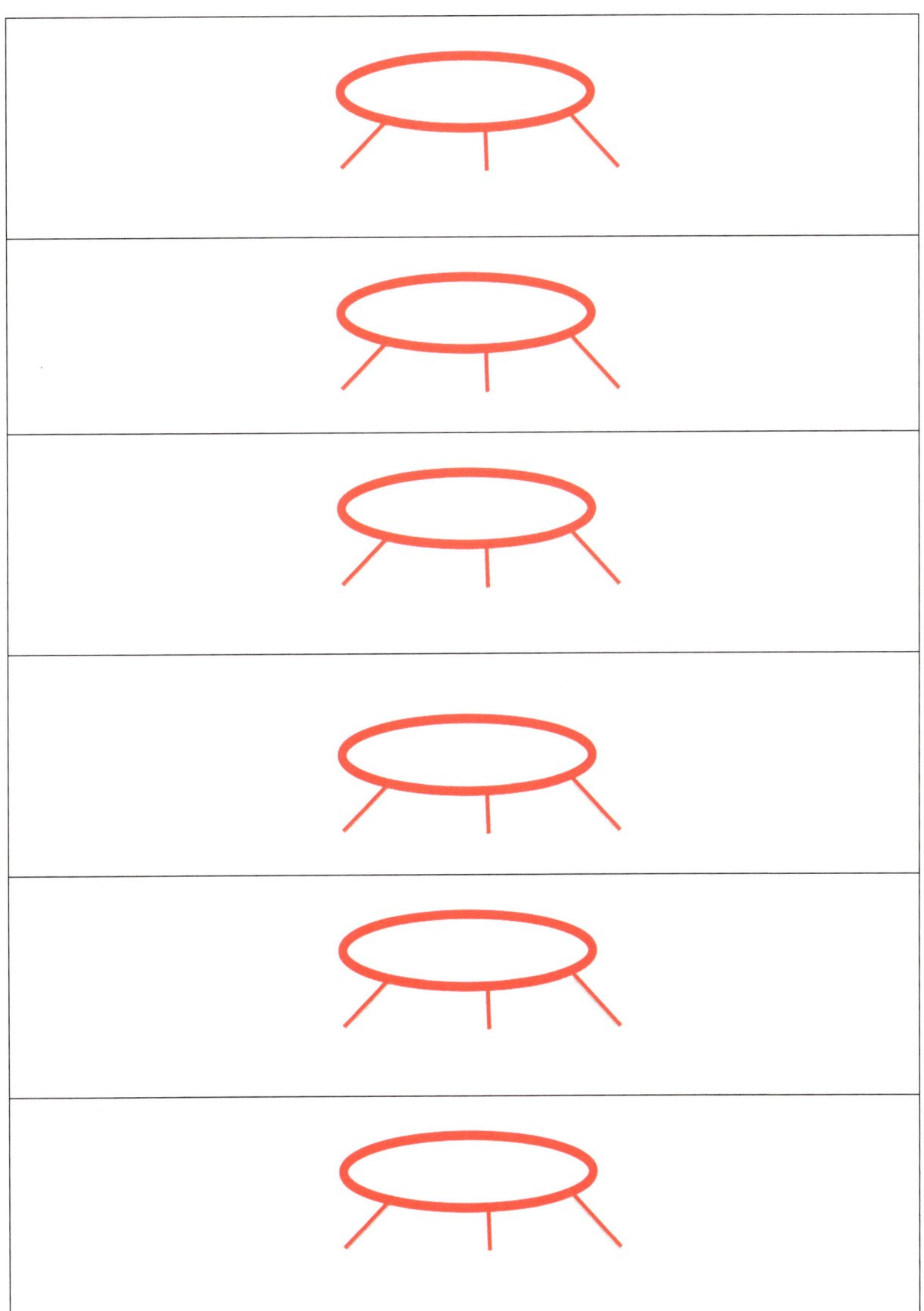

L1 Review A

Place in alphabetical order

1. **impossible**
2. **fraction**
3. **physician**
4. **enjoyment**
5. **avoid**
6. **nonsense**

L1 Review B

Unscramble the words

1. shpaiyicn - _____
2. imseobpsli - _____
3. tioacnrf - _____
4. tnomenyej - _____
5. vioda - _____
6. sennsoen - _____

L1 Test

Fill in the blanks.

1. **enjoyment** _____

2. **impossible** - _____

3. **nonsense** - _____

4. _____ - part of a whole

5. _____ - a person trained to treat illness; a doctor

6. _____ - to stay away from ; to keep out of the way of ; to dodge

Lesson 2

1. **pitcher** - a container pouring liquid
2. **nearby** - a short distance away
3. **subzero** - below zero
4. **expensive** - costly; high in price
5. **detail** - trait or part of someone or something
6. **destroy** - to ruin; to wreck

L2 MEANINGFUL SENTENCES

Make a word web and write a meaningful sentence for each word in this lesson. Never try to write a meaningful sentence without first creating a word web. The word web is a part of the process for helping you transfer your new knowledge into your long-term memory. This page is your rough draft of the assignment. On a piece of notebook paper, number one-ten and rewrite each meaningful sentence. Highlight the vocabulary word pink, the context clue yellow and the definition blue. You will turn the final draft in for grading.

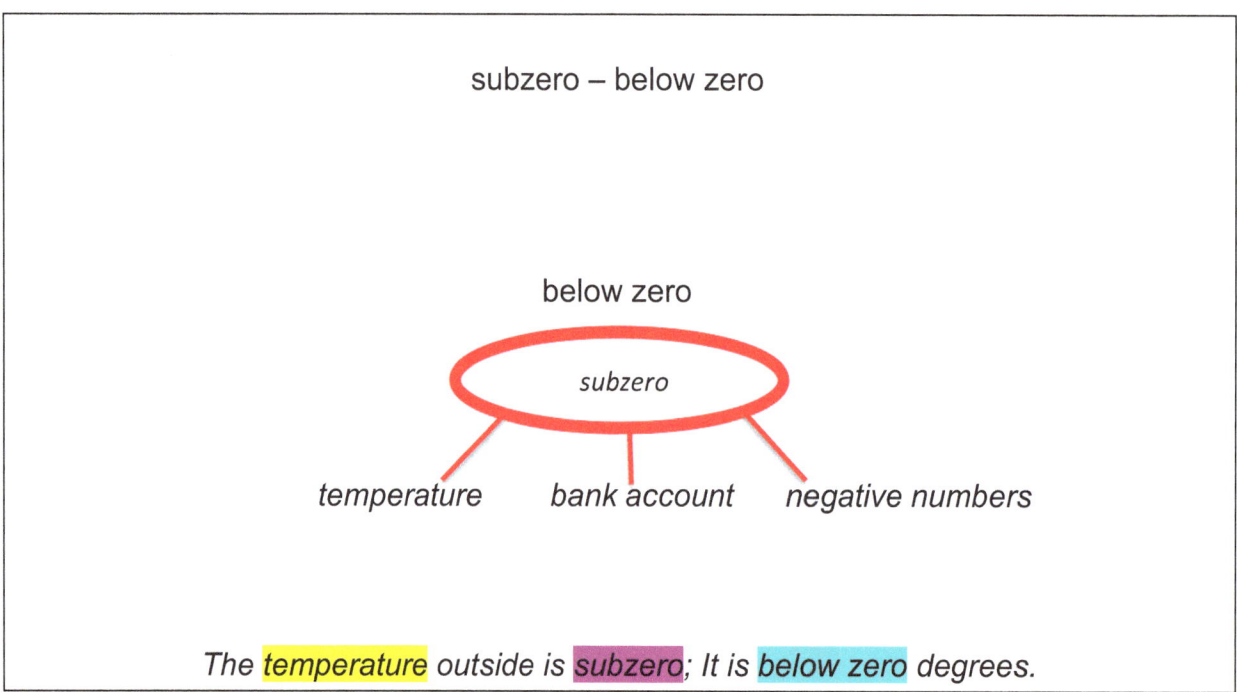

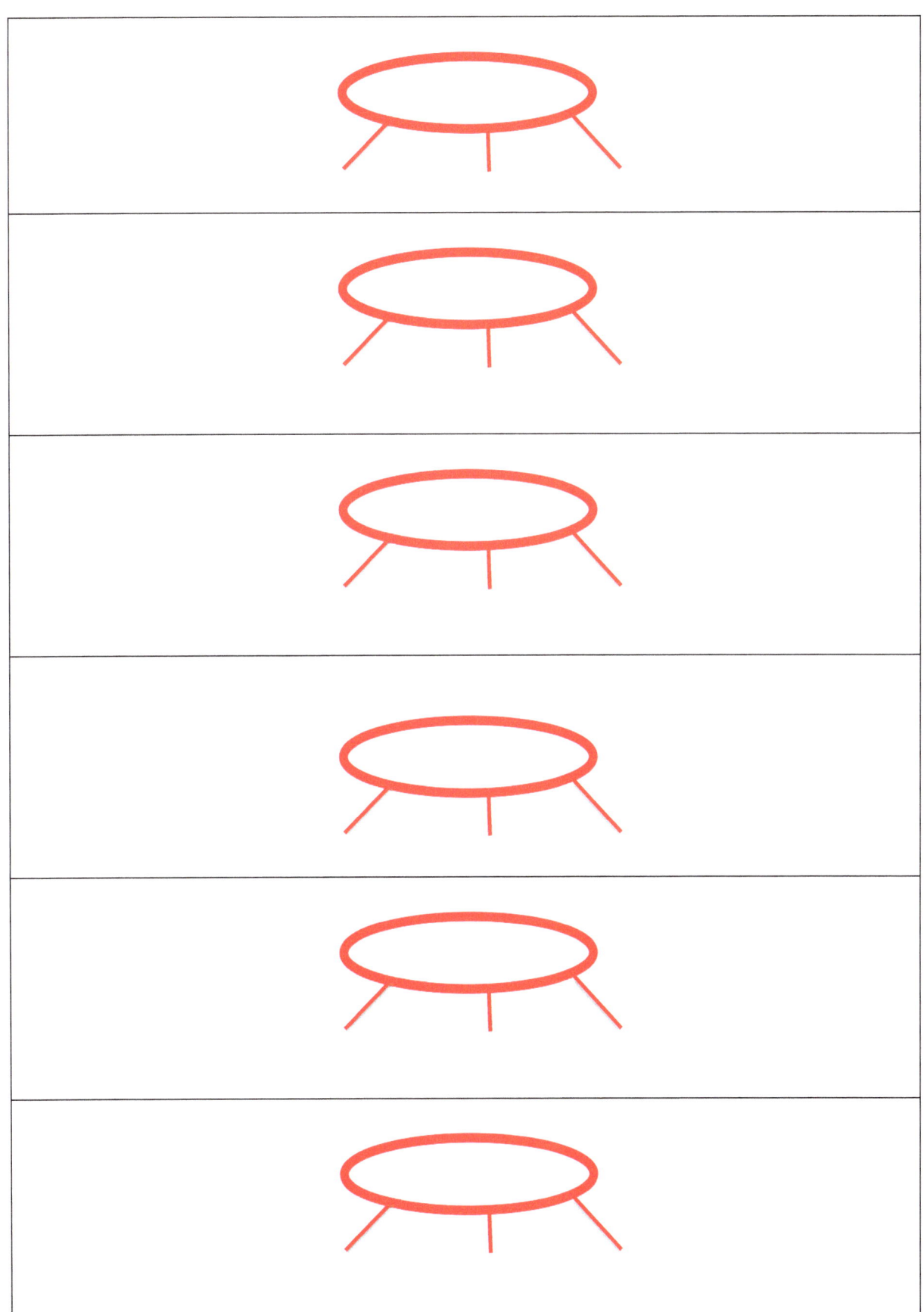

L2 Review A

Place in alphabetical order

1. **pitcher**
2. **nearby**
3. **subzero**
4. **expensive**
5. **detail**
6. **destroy**

L2 Review B

Unscramble the words.

1. litaed - _____
2. srteyod - _____
3. esrozbu - _____
4. epxisveen - _____
5. ipcerht - _____
6. rnbyae - _____

L2 Test

Fill in the blanks.

1. _____ - trait or part of someone or something

2. _____ - to ruin; to wreck

3. _____ - below zero

4. expensive - _____

5. pitcher - _____

6. nearby - _____

Lesson 3

1. **population** - the number of people living in a place
2. **dialogue** - a conversation between two or more characters
3. **startle** - to alarm ; frighten
4. **spectacular** - marvelous; wonderful ; breathtaking
5. **marvelous** - wonderful; astonishing
6. **corporation** - a business

L3 MEANINGFUL SENTENCES

Make a word web and write a meaningful sentence for each word in this lesson. Never try to write a meaningful sentence without first creating a word web. The word web is a part of the process for helping you transfer your new knowledge into your long-term memory. This page is your rough draft of the assignment. On a piece of notebook paper, number one-ten and rewrite each meaningful sentence. Highlight the vocabulary word pink, the context clue yellow and the definition blue. You will turn the final draft in for grading.

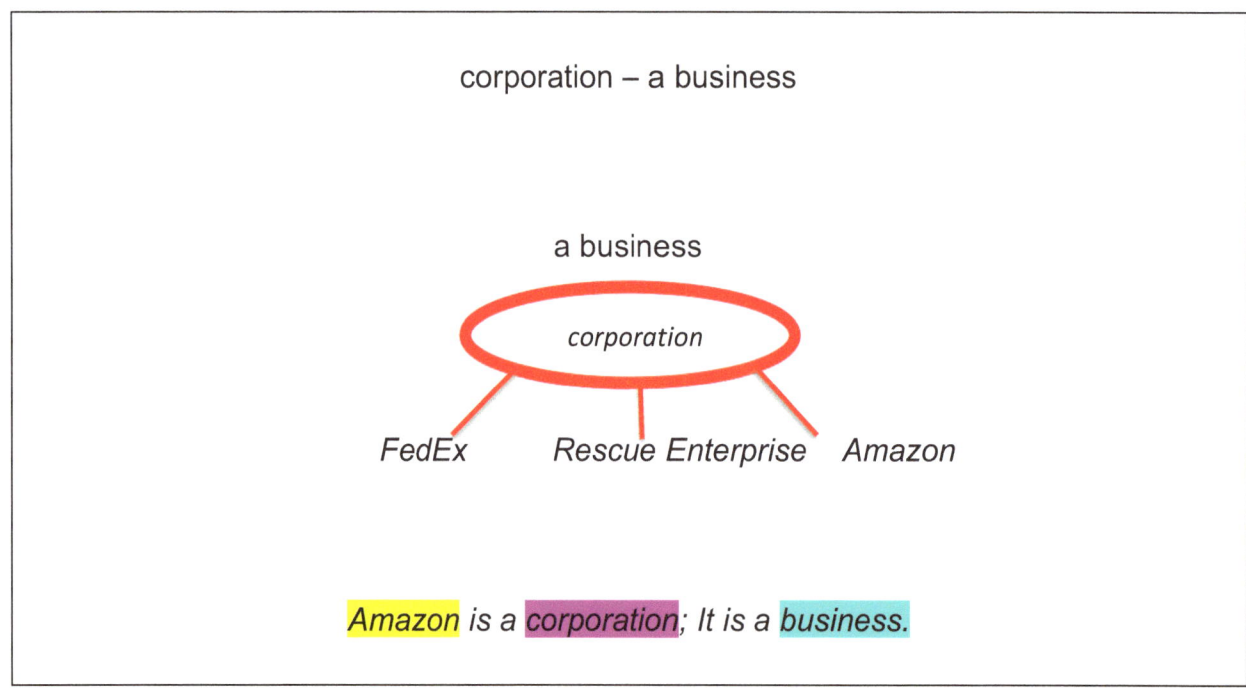

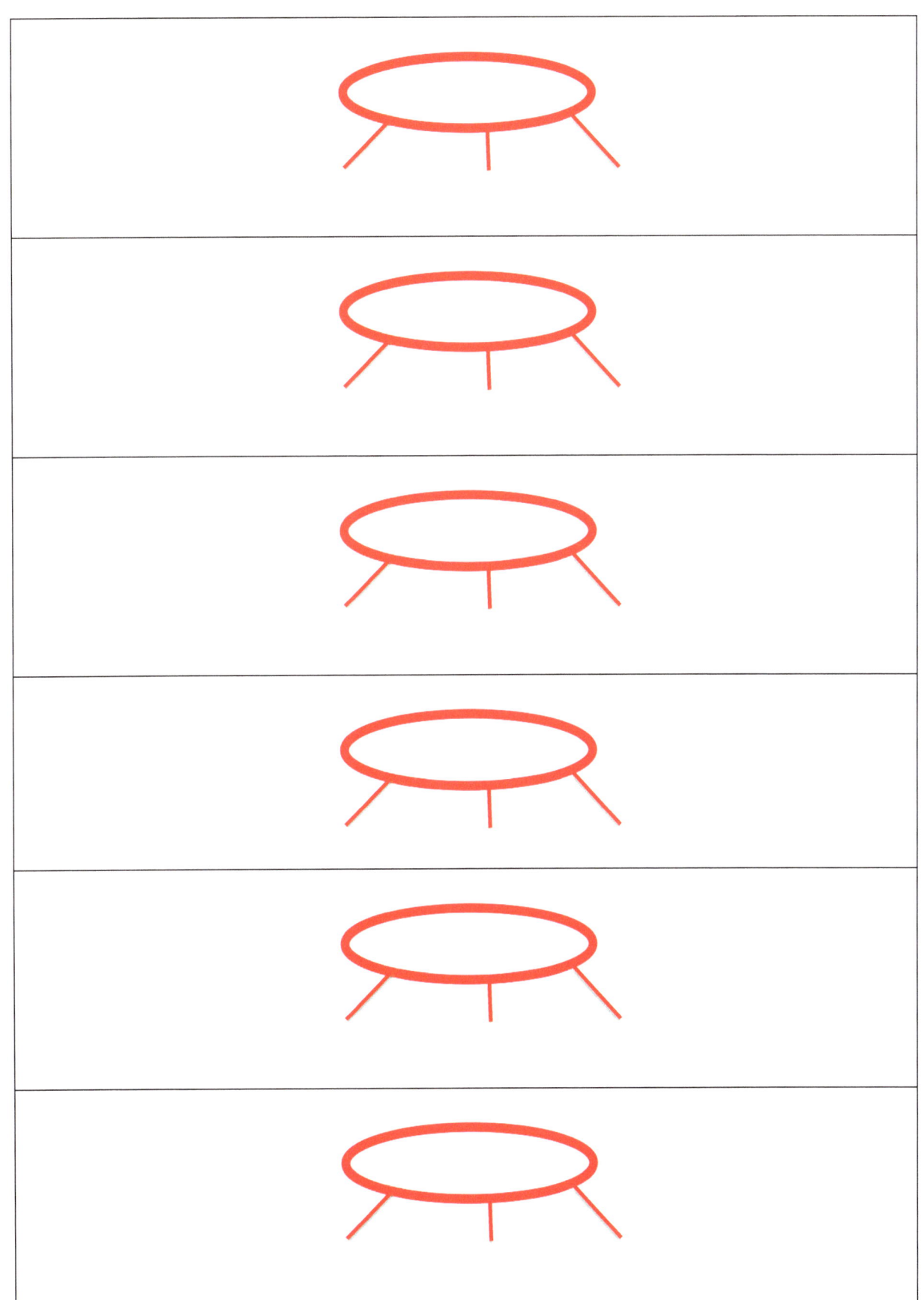

L3 Review A

Place in alphabetical order.

1. **population**
2. **dialogue**
3. **startle**
4. **spectacular**
5. **marvelous**
6. **corporation**

L3 Review B

Unscramble the words.

1. ildeaugo - _____
2. pustcelcraa - _____
3. itpnuooapl - _____
4. aslttre - _____
5. vmeulsroa - _____
6. prcoorntoai - _____

L3 Test

Fill in the blanks.

1. _____ -to alarm ; frighten

2. _____ - marvelous; wonderful ; breathtaking

3. _____ - a conversation between two or more characters

4. marvelous - _____

5. corporation - _____

6. population - _____

Lesson 4

1. **dangerous** - unsafe; harmful
2. **coma** - an unconscious state
3. **homework** - work for school that is done at home
4. **plot** - a series of events that move the story forward
5. **country** - a nation
6. **research** - careful study or investigation of a topic

L4 MEANINGFUL SENTENCES

Make a word web and write a meaningful sentence for each word in this lesson. Never try to write a meaningful sentence without first creating a word web. The word web is a part of the process for helping you transfer your new knowledge into your long-term memory. This page is your rough draft of the assignment. On a piece of notebook paper, number one-ten and rewrite each meaningful sentence. Highlight the vocabulary word pink, the context clue yellow and the definition blue. You will turn the final draft in for grading.

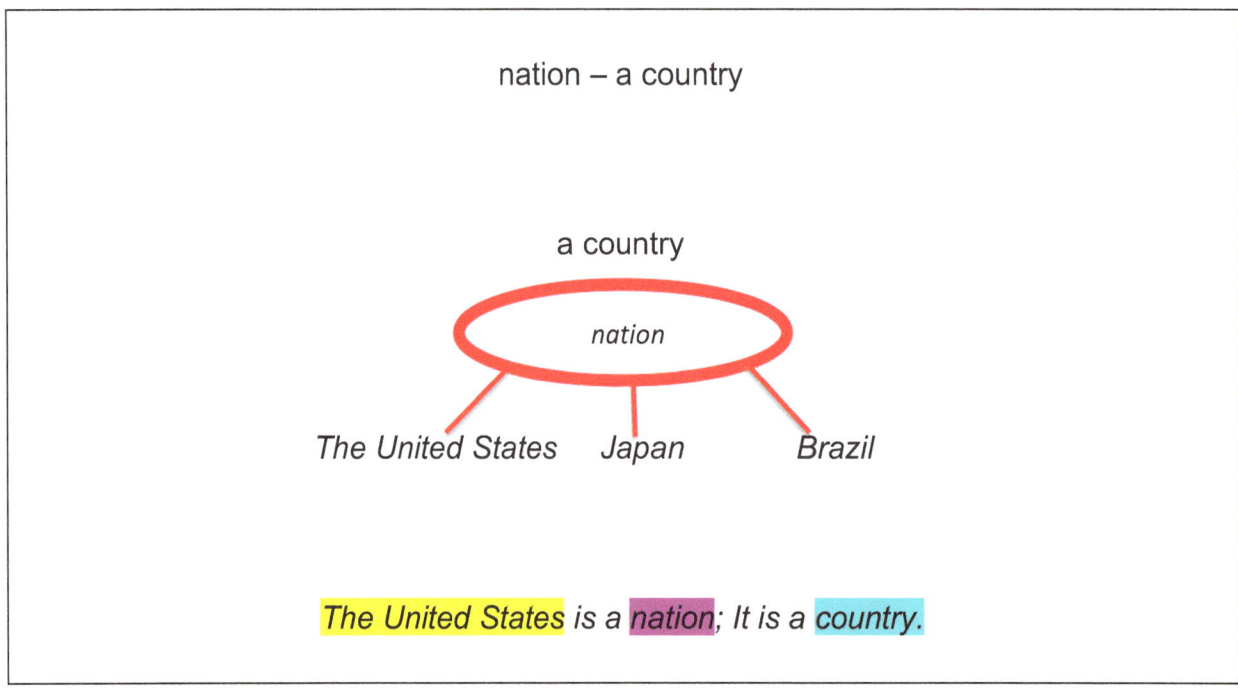

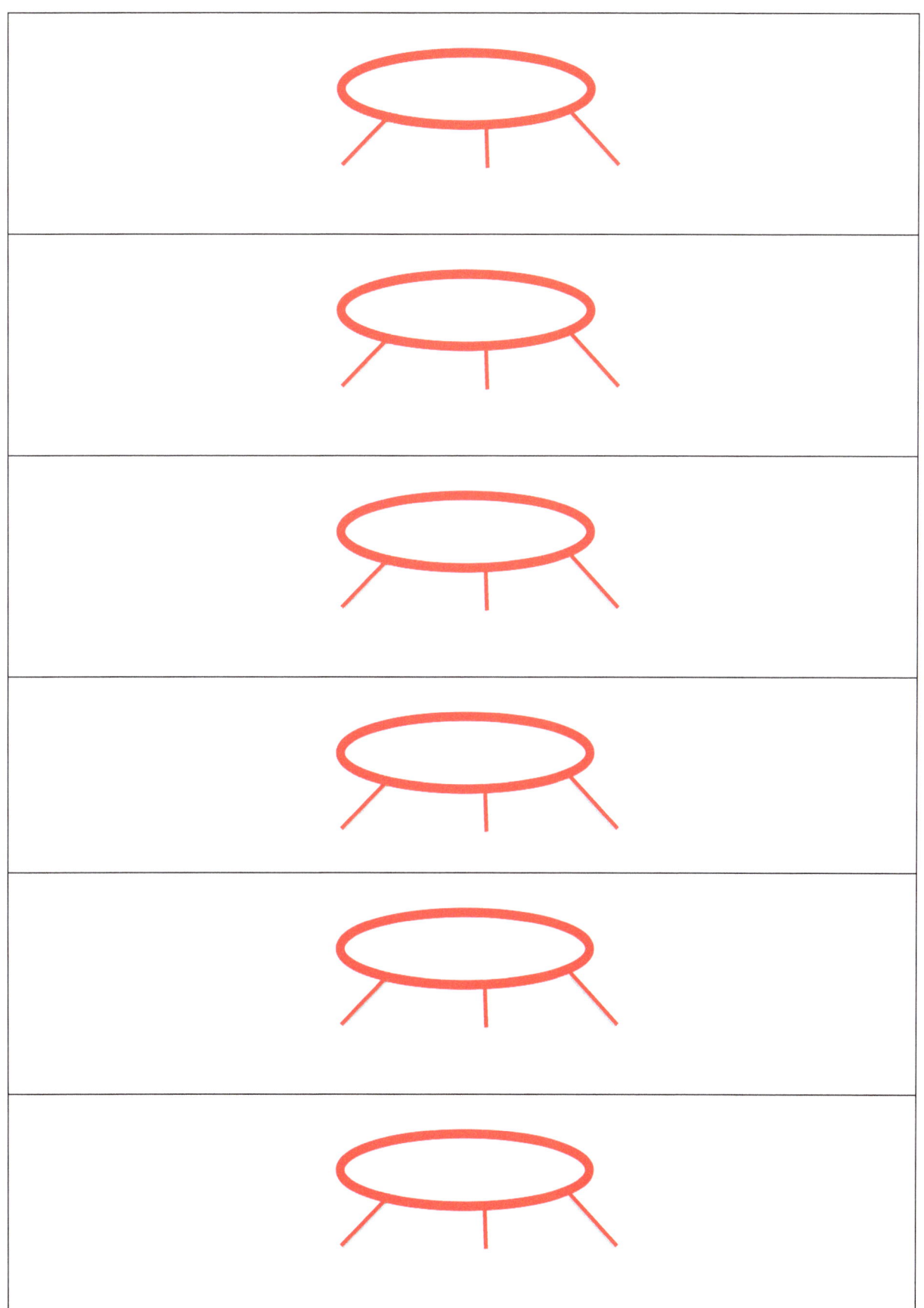

L4 Review A

Place in alphabetical order.

1. **dangerous**
2. **coma**
3. **homework**
4. **plot**
5. **country**
6. **research**

L4 Review B

Unscramble the words.

1. songdaeur - _____
2. potl - _____
3. ocma - _____
4. creasehr - _____
5. untryco - _____
6. orheomkw - _____

L4 Test

Fill in the blanks.

1. _____ - work for school that is done at home

2. _____ - unsafe; harmful

3. _____ - an unconscious state

4. plot - _____

5. research - _____

6. country - _____

Lesson 5

1. **jog** - to run at a slow pace
2. **different** - not alike; not like others; various
3. **impatient** - restless; not able to put up with delay
4. **way** - path; road ; course
5. **brash** - hasty; rash; unthinking
6. **pupil** - a student

L5 MEANINGFUL SENTENCES

Make a word web and write a meaningful sentence for each word in this lesson. Never try to write a meaningful sentence without first creating a word web. The word web is a part of the process for helping you transfer your new knowledge into your long-term memory. This page is your rough draft of the assignment. On a piece of notebook paper, number one-ten and rewrite each meaningful sentence. Highlight the vocabulary word pink, the context clue yellow and the definition blue. You will turn the final draft in for grading.

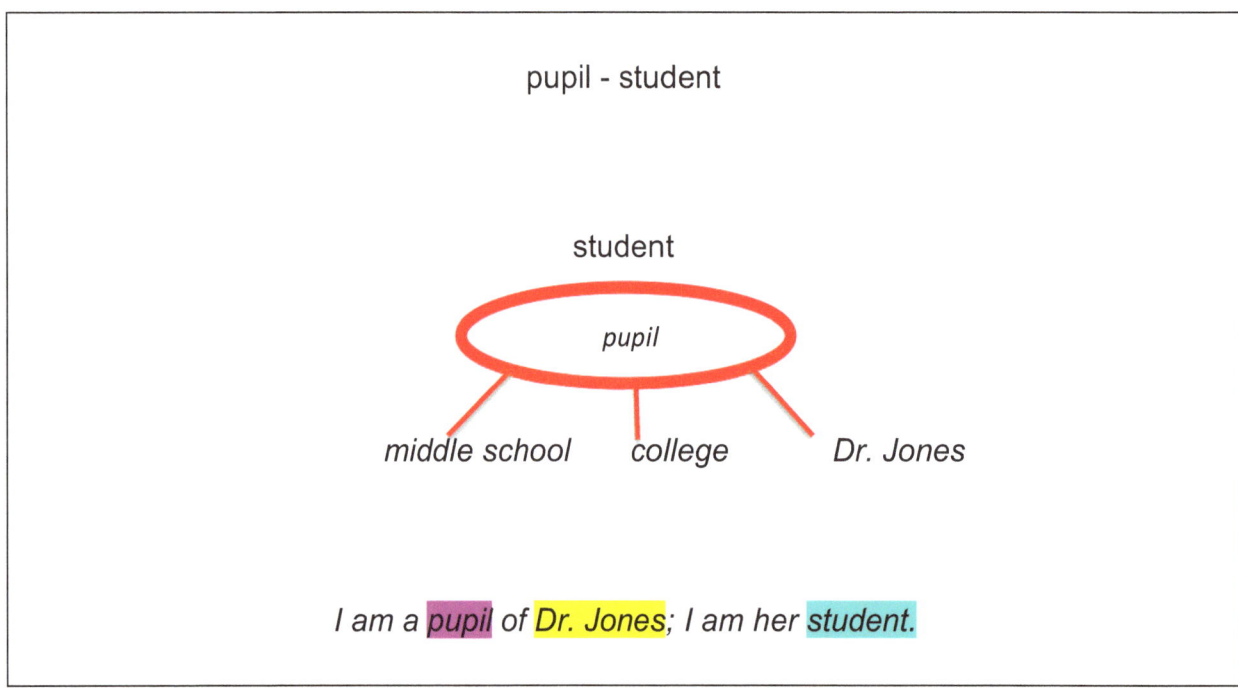

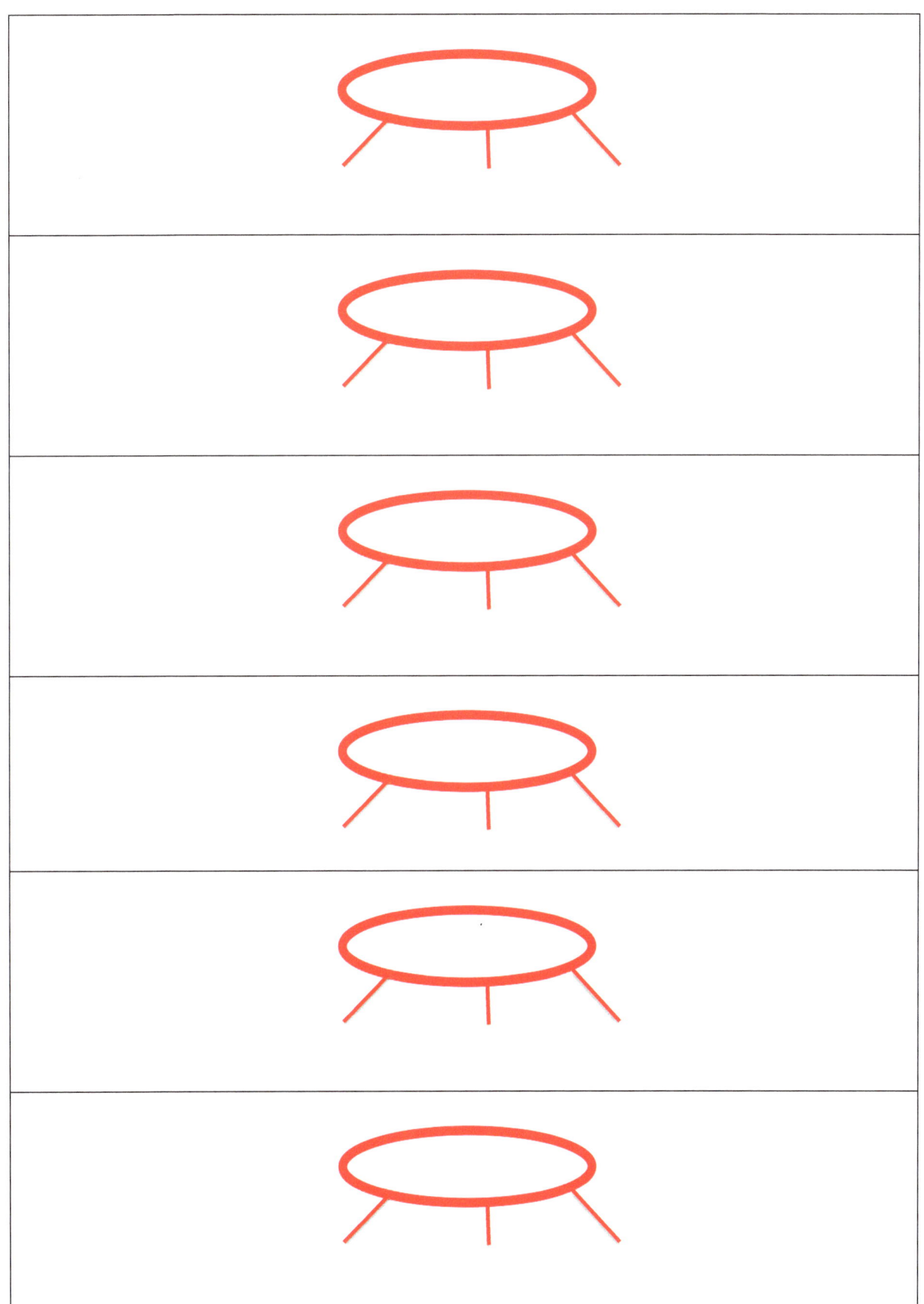

L5 Review A

Place in alphabetical order.

1. **jog**
2. **different**
3. **impatient**
4. **way**
5. **brash**
6. **pupil**

L5 Review B

Unscramble the words.

1. piplu - _____
2. feefdntri - _____
3. abrhs - _____
4. aptiteimn - _____
5. jgo - _____
6. ayw - _____

L5 Test

1. _____ - not alike; not like others; various

2. _____ - hasty; rash; unthinking

3. _____ - path; road ; course

4. pupil - _____

5. impatient - _____

6. jog - _____

Lesson 6

1. **underground** - beneath the surface of the earth
2. **smash** - to break violently; to shatter
3. **delightful** - enjoyable ; pleasant
4. **exotic** - unfamiliar; strange; unusual
5. **tornado** - a violent storm with winds in the shape of a funnel ; whirlwind
6. **misspell** - to spell incorrectly

L6 MEANINGFUL SENTENCES

Make a word web and write a meaningful sentence for each word in this lesson. Never try to write a meaningful sentence without first creating a word web. The word web is a part of the process for helping you transfer your new knowledge into your long-term memory. This page is your rough draft of the assignment. On a piece of notebook paper, number one-ten and rewrite each meaningful sentence. Highlight the vocabulary word pink, the context clue yellow and the definition blue. You will turn the final draft in for grading.

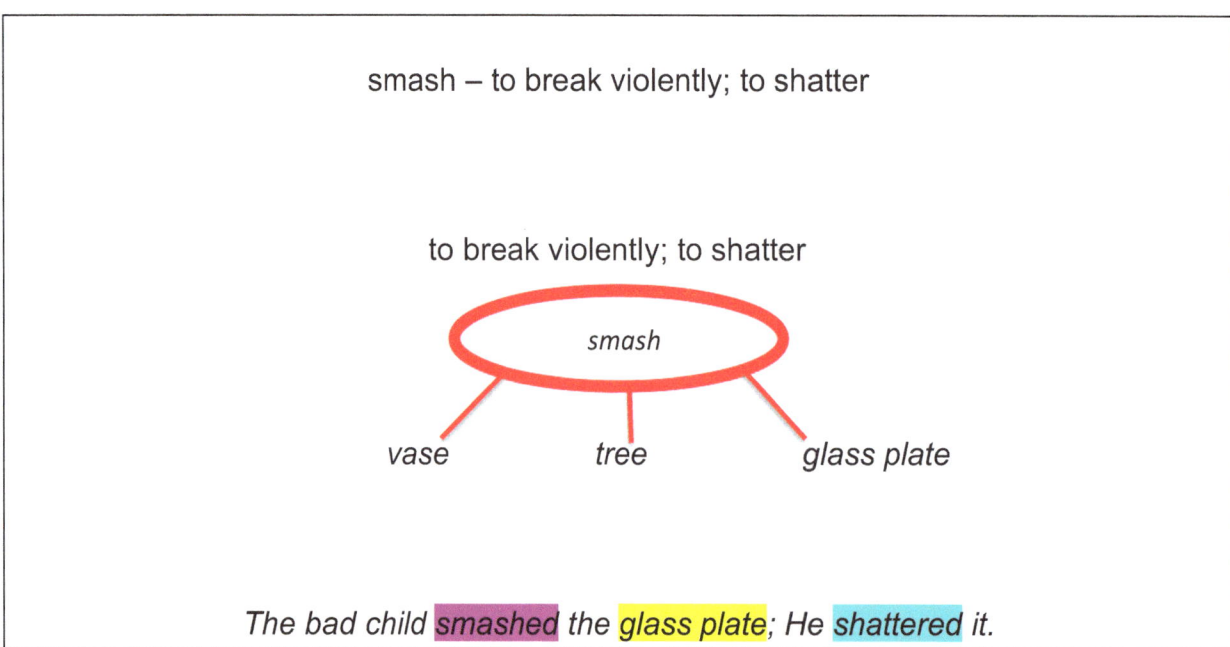

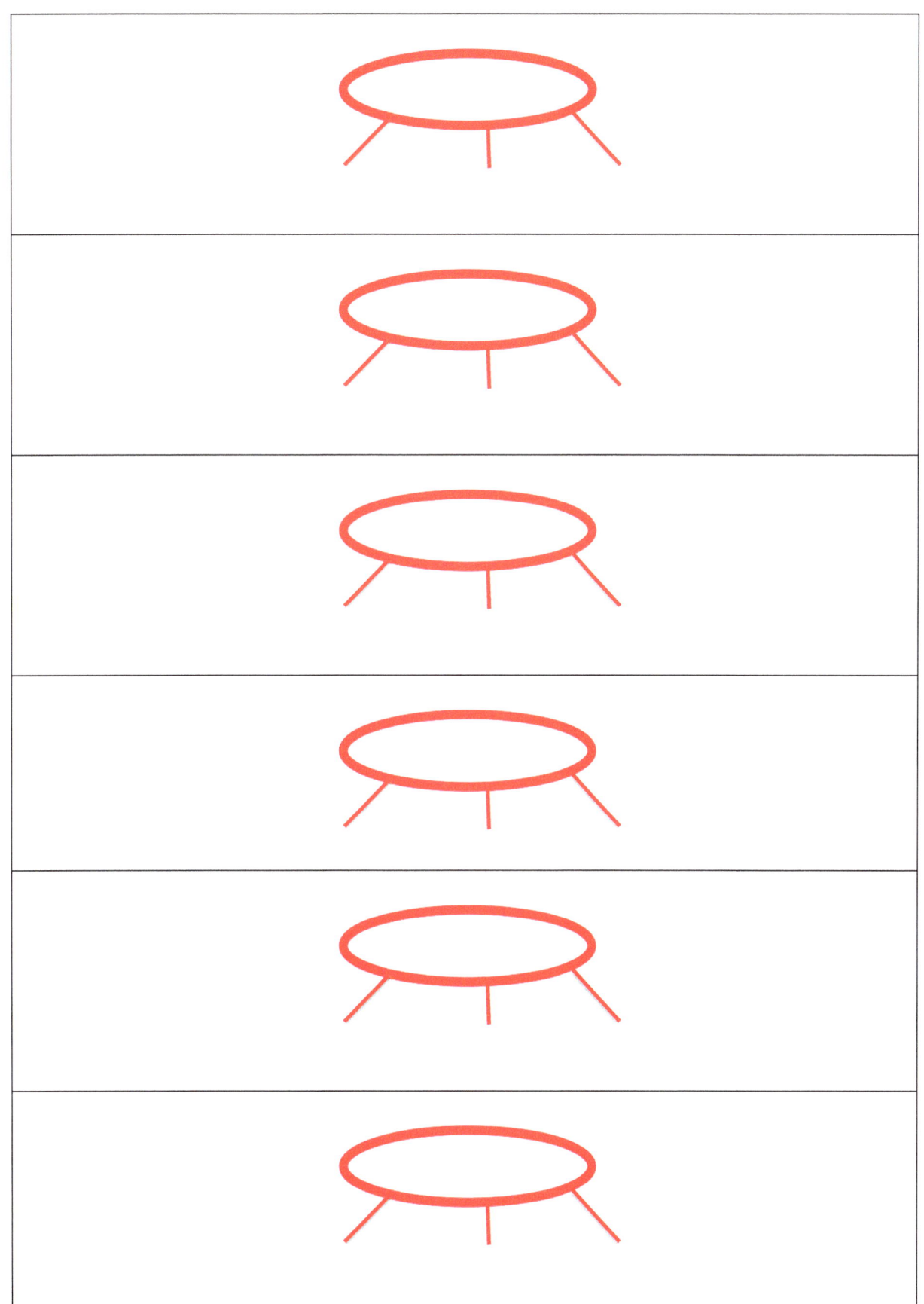

L6 Review A

Place in alphabetical order.

1. **underground**
2. **smash**
3. **delightful**
4. **exotic**
5. **tornado**
6. **misspell**

L6 Review B

Unscramble the words

1. urnendrgduo - _____
2. mislples - _____
3. lgihtudlfe - _____
4. danotor - _____
5. itcexo - _____
6. assmh - _____

L6 Test

1. _____ - to break violently; to shatter

2. _____ - a violent storm with winds in the shape of a funnel ; whirlwind

3. _____ - unfamiliar; strange; unusual

4. delightful - _____

5. misspell -_____

6. underground - _____

Lesson 7

1. **duck** - to dip or dodge quickly
2. **vigorous** - energetic ; intense
3. **solution** - an answer; an explanation
4. **expect** - to look for a thing to happen
5. **drowsy** - sleepy; half-asleep
6. **equal** - the same amount , quantity, or value

L7 MEANINGFUL SENTENCES

Make a word web and write a meaningful sentence for each word in this lesson. Never try to write a meaningful sentence without first creating a word web. The word web is a part of the process for helping you transfer your new knowledge into your long-term memory. This page is your rough draft of the assignment. On a piece of notebook paper, number one-ten and rewrite each meaningful sentence. Highlight the vocabulary word pink, the context clue yellow and the definition blue. You will turn the final draft in for grading.

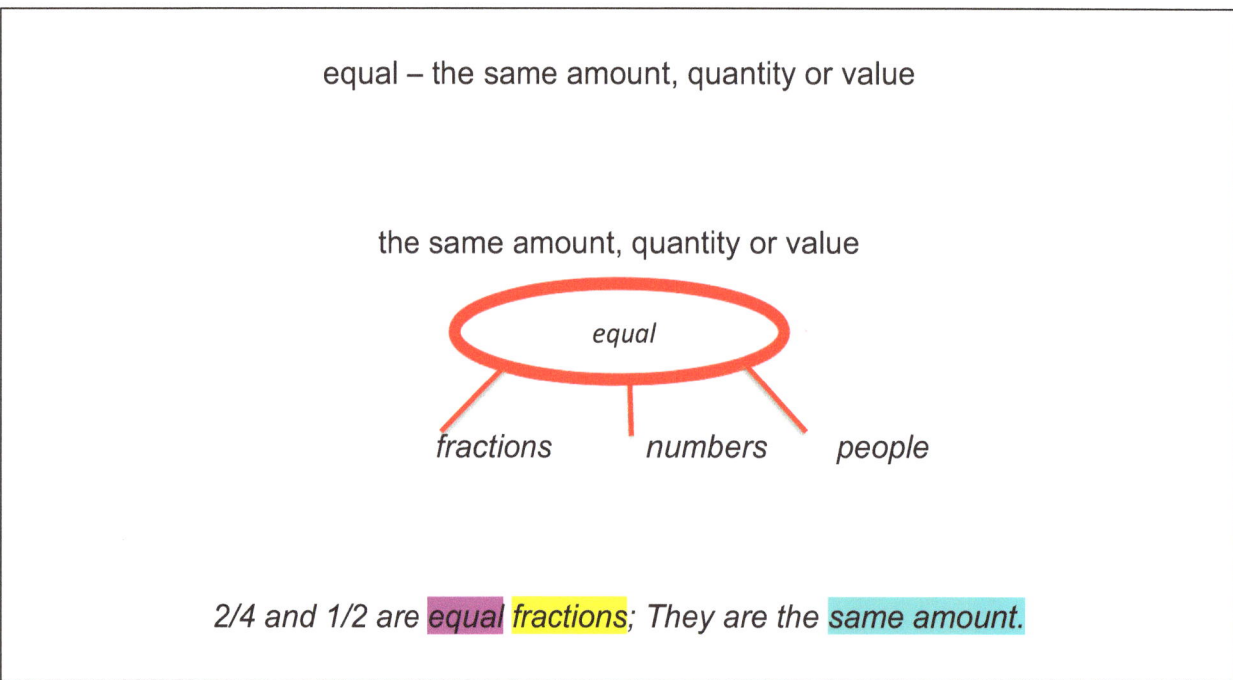

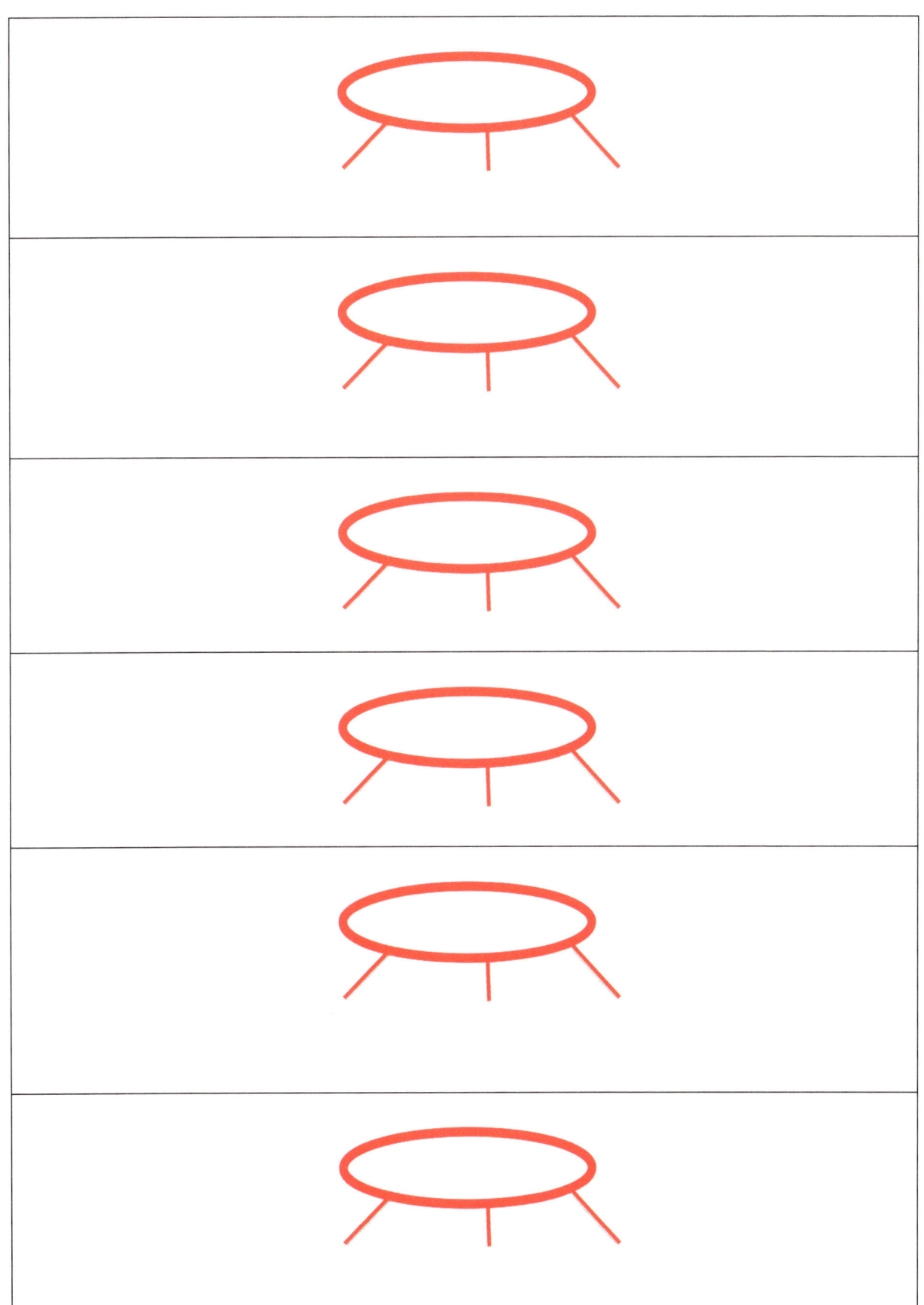

L7 Review A

Place in alphabetical order.

1. **duck**
2. **vigorous**
3. **solution**
4. **expect**
5. **drowsy**
6. **equal**

L7 Review B

Unscramble the words.

1. execpt - _____
2. ordysw - _____
3. oorugsiv - _____
4. touonlsi - _____
5. qulea - _____
6. cudk - _____

L7 Test

1. _____ - to look for a thing to happen

2. _____ - energetic ; intense

3. _____ - the same amount, quantity, or value

4. drowsy - _____

5. duck - _____

6. solution - _____

Lesson 8

1. **justice** - fairness

2. **childish** - behaving like a child ; immature; silly

3. **sell** - to exchange money

4. **splurge** - to spend excessively

5. **author** - a writer

6. **define** - to state the meaning of ; to describe

L8 MEANINGFUL SENTENCES

Make a word web and write a meaningful sentence for each word in this lesson. Never try to write a meaningful sentence without first creating a word web. The word web is a part of the process for helping you transfer your new knowledge into your long-term memory. This page is your rough draft of the assignment. On a piece of notebook paper, number one-ten and rewrite each meaningful sentence. Highlight the vocabulary word pink, the context clue yellow and the definition blue. You will turn the final draft in for grading.

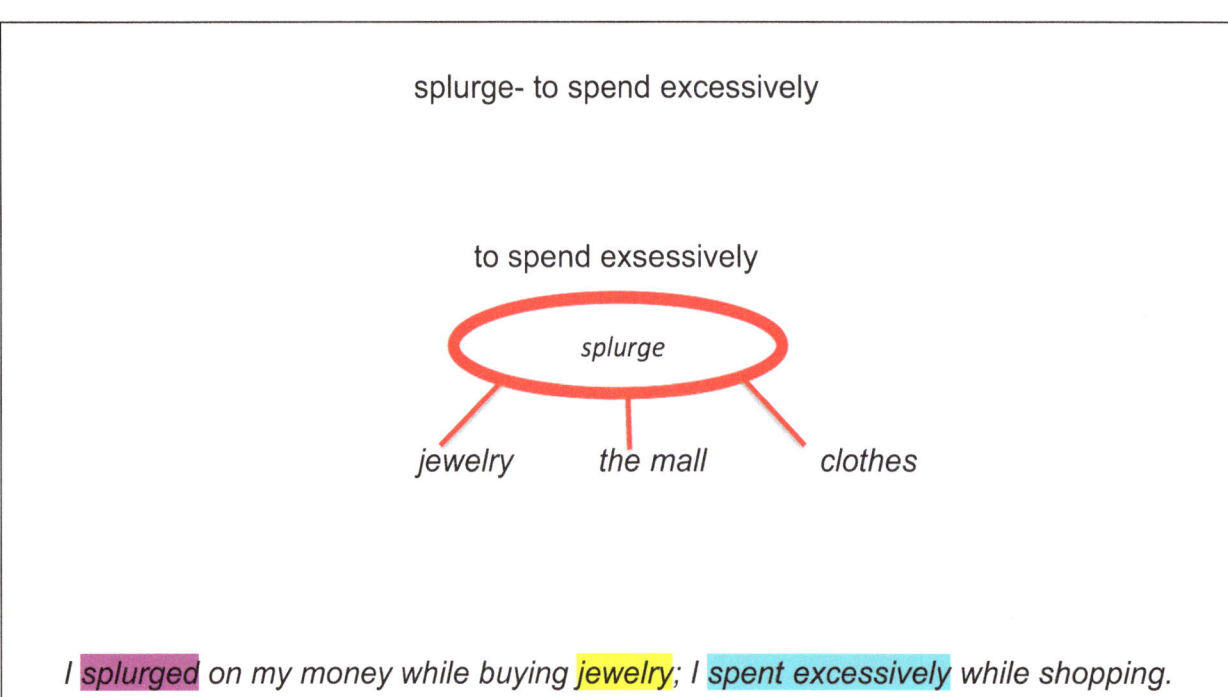

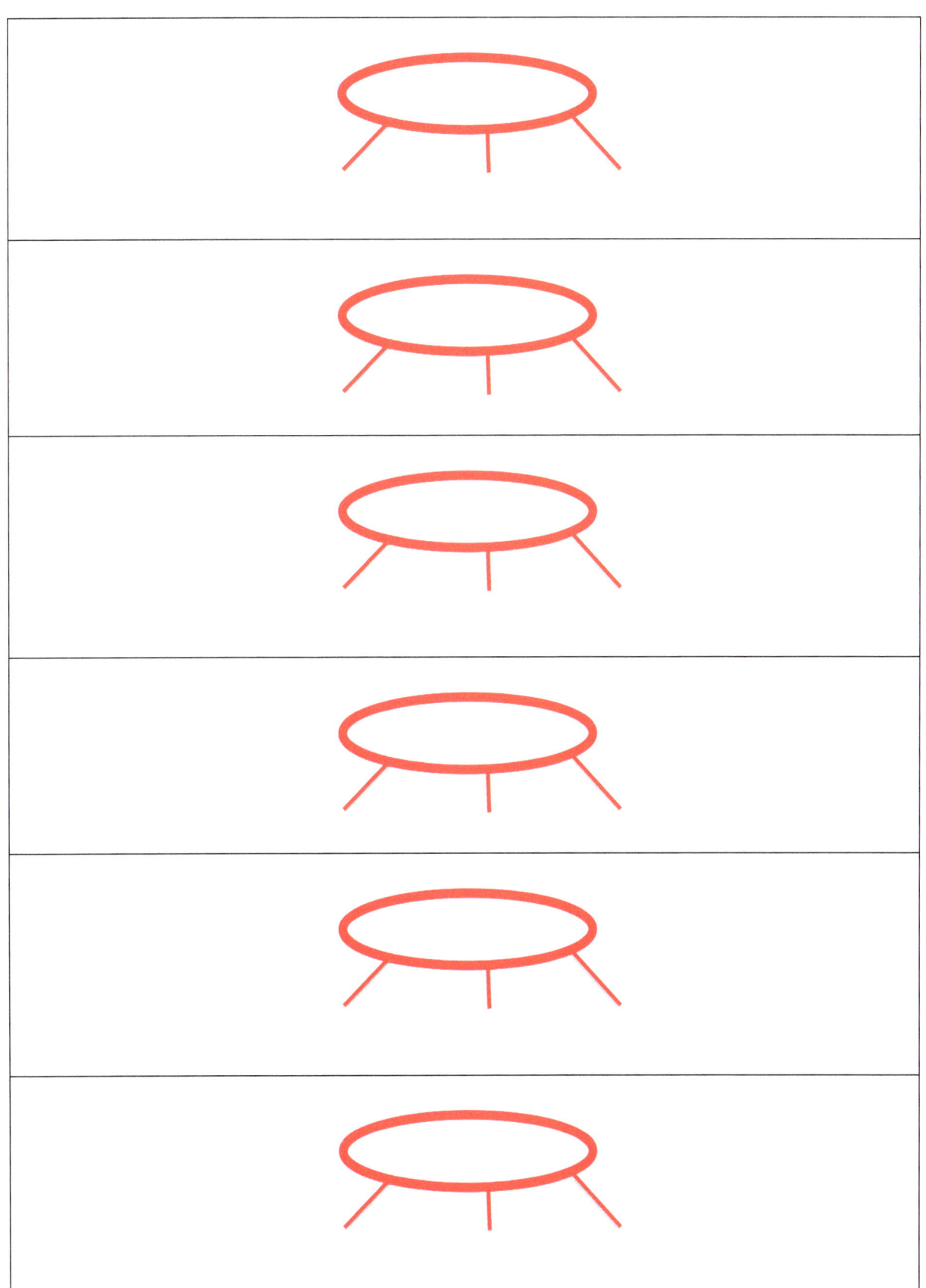

L8 Review A

Place in alphabetical order.

1. **justice**
2. **childish**
3. **sell**
4. **splurge**
5. **author**
6. **define**

L8 Review B

Unscramble the words

1. aurtoh - _____
2. cdlisihh - _____
3. fnedei - _____
4. stuejic - _____
5. lesl - _____
6. leprusg - _____

L8 Test

1. _____ - a writer

2. _____ - fairness

3. _____ - to spend excessively

4. sell - _____

5. define - _____

6. childish - _____

Lesson 9

1. **obey** - to follow orders

2. **rage** - anger ; fury; wrath

3. **bandit** - an outlaw; a robber; a thief

4. **monarch** - the rule of a nation; a king or queen

5. **common** - usual ; frequent

6. **revise** - rewrite; change ; alter

L9 MEANINGFUL SENTENCES

Make a word web and write a meaningful sentence for each word in this lesson. Never try to write a meaningful sentence without first creating a word web. The word web is a part of the process for helping you transfer your new knowledge into your long-term memory. This page is your rough draft of the assignment. On a piece of notebook paper, number one-ten and rewrite each meaningful sentence. Highlight the vocabulary word pink, the context clue yellow and the definition blue. You will turn the final draft in for grading.

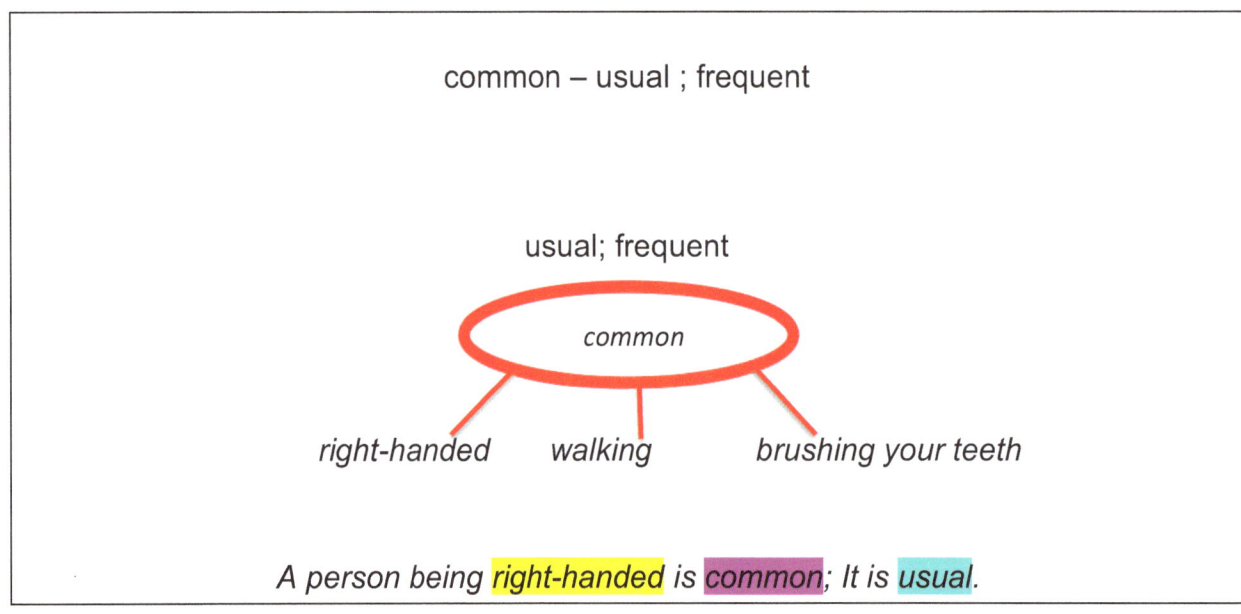

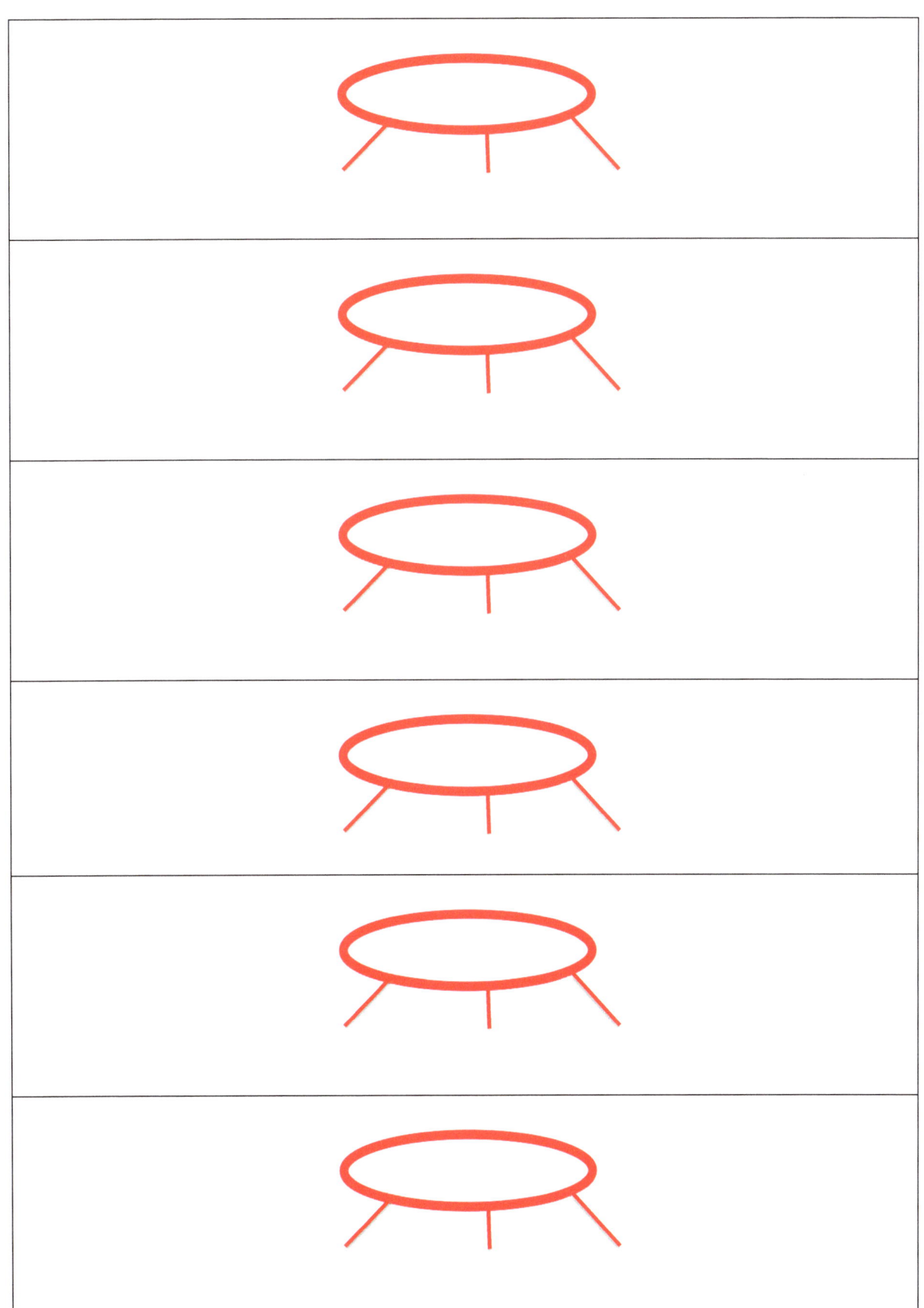

L9 Review A

Place in alphabetical order.

1. **obey**
2. **rage**
3. **bandit**
4. **monarch**
5. **common**
6. **revise**

L9 Review B

Unscramble the words

1. sveeri - _____
2. oeyb - _____
3. moconm - _____
4. gare - _____
5. ocamrnh - _____
6. iabndt - _____

L9 Test

1. _____ - the rule of a nation; a king or queen

2. _____ - rewrite; change; alter

3. _____ - usual; frequent

4. obey - _____

5. bandit - _____

6. rage - _____

TRIMESTER 1 EXAM

1. justice - _____
2. tornado - _____
3. sell - _____
4. delightful - _____
5. subzero - _____
6. monarch - _____
7. misspell - _____
8. revise - _____
9. define - _____
10. impatient - _____
11. brash - _____
12. nonsense - _____
13. avoid - _____
14. common - _____
15. startle - _____
16. expensive - _____
17. nearby -_____
18. detail - _____
19. country - _____
20. rage - _____
21. destroy -_____
22. smash - _____
23. pupil - _____

24. impossible - _____

25. dangerous - _____

26. corporation - _____

27. plot - _____

28. duck - _____

29. underground - _____

30. vigorous - _____

31. population - _____

32. expect - _____

33. pitcher - _____

34. dialogue - _____

35. coma - _____

36. author - _____

37. enjoyment - _____

38. splurge - _____

39. research - _____

40. obey - _____

41. jog - _____

42. homework - _____

43. exotic - _____

44. childish - _____

45. fraction - _____

46. drowsy - _____

47. different - _____

48. bandit - _____

49. solution - _____

Lesson 10

1. **yard** - 36 inches

2. **loose** - not tight

3. **quit** - to stop

4. **aquatic** - relating to the water

5. **matriarch** - a woman who rules or leads a family or clan

6. **apology** - words saying that a person is sorry

L10 MEANINGFUL SENTENCES

Make a word web and write a meaningful sentence for each word in this lesson. Never try to write a meaningful sentence without first creating a word web. The word web is a part of the process for helping you transfer your new knowledge into your long-term memory. This page is your rough draft of the assignment. On a piece of notebook paper, number one-ten and rewrite each meaningful sentence. Highlight the vocabulary word pink, the context clue yellow and the definition blue. You will turn the final draft in for grading.

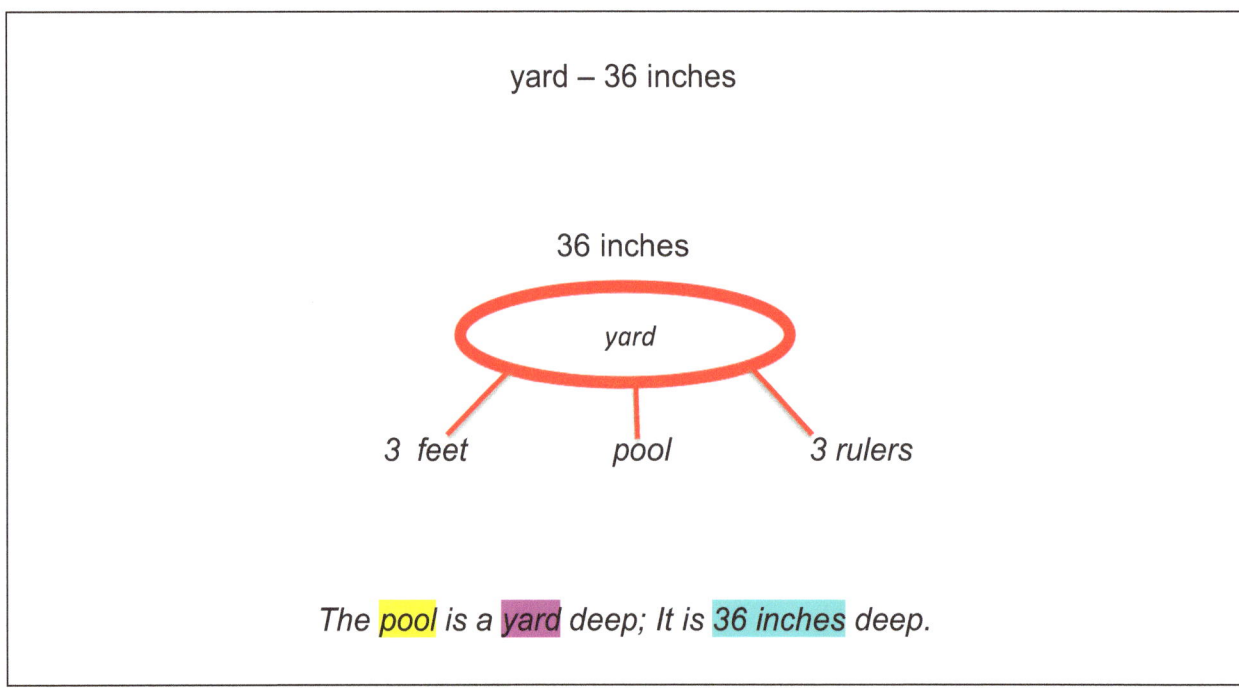

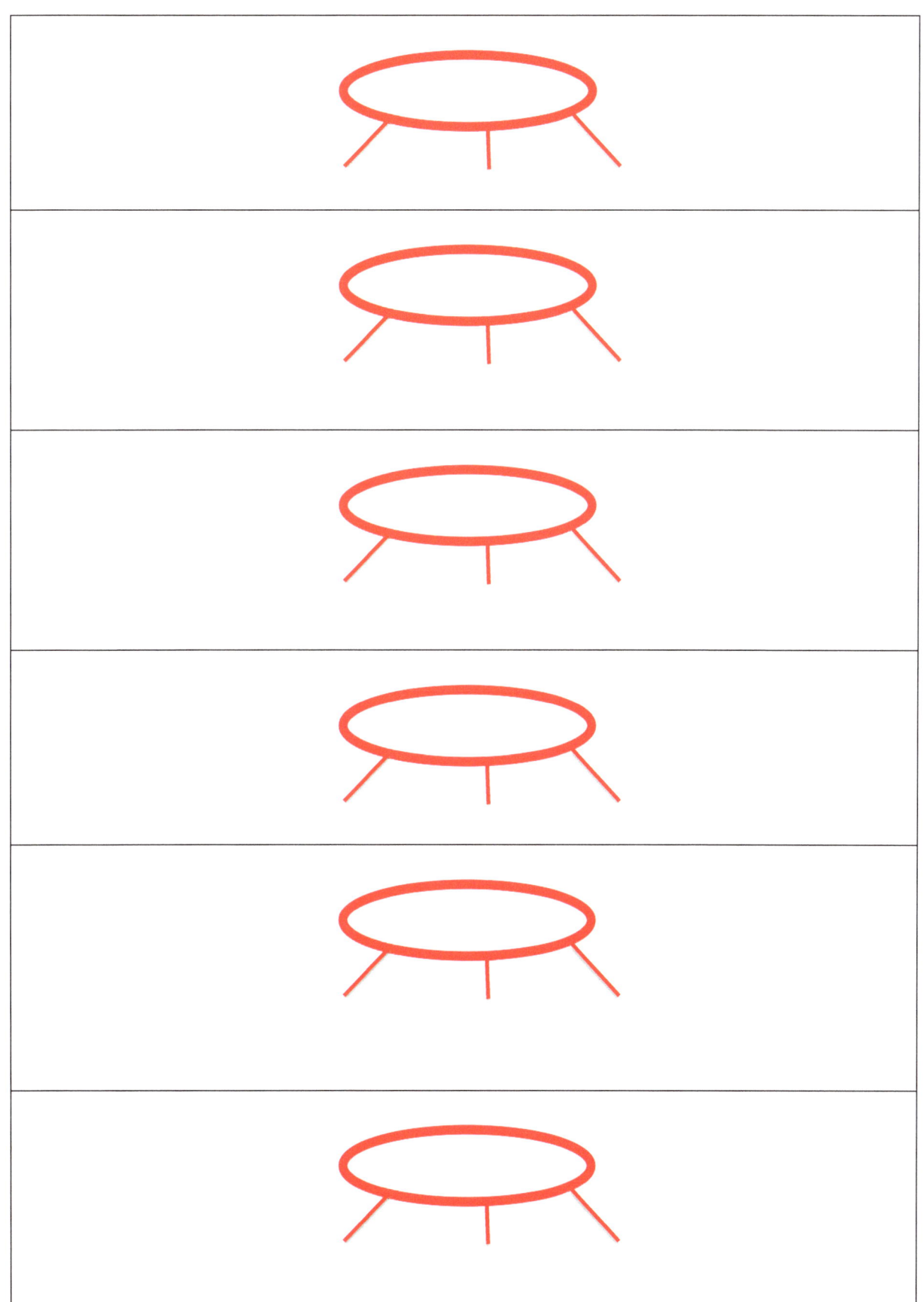

L10 Review A

Place in alphabetical order.

1. **yard**
2. **loose**
3. **quit**
4. **aquatic**
5. **matriarch**
6. **apology**

L10 Review B

Unscramble the words

1. uitq - _____
2. soloe - _____
3. yrad - _____
4. mihatcrar - _____
5. uciqaat - _____
6. olgpayo - _____

L10 Test

1. _____ - words saying that a person is sorry

2. _____ - to stop

3. _____ - relating to the water

4. matriarch - _____

5. loose - _____

6. yard - _____

Lesson 11

1. **desert** - a dry wasteland

2. **tire** - a rubber placed around a wheel

3. **famous** - well known; honored

4. **break** - to come apart; to separate into pieces

5. **divide** - separate; split

6. **whole** - complete ; entire

L11 MEANINGFUL SENTENCES

Make a word web and write a meaningful sentence for each word in this lesson. Never try to write a meaningful sentence without first creating a word web. The word web is a part of the process for helping you transfer your new knowledge into your long-term memory. This page is your rough draft of the assignment. On a piece of notebook paper, number one-ten and rewrite each meaningful sentence. Highlight the vocabulary word pink, the context clue yellow and the definition blue. You will turn the final draft in for grading.

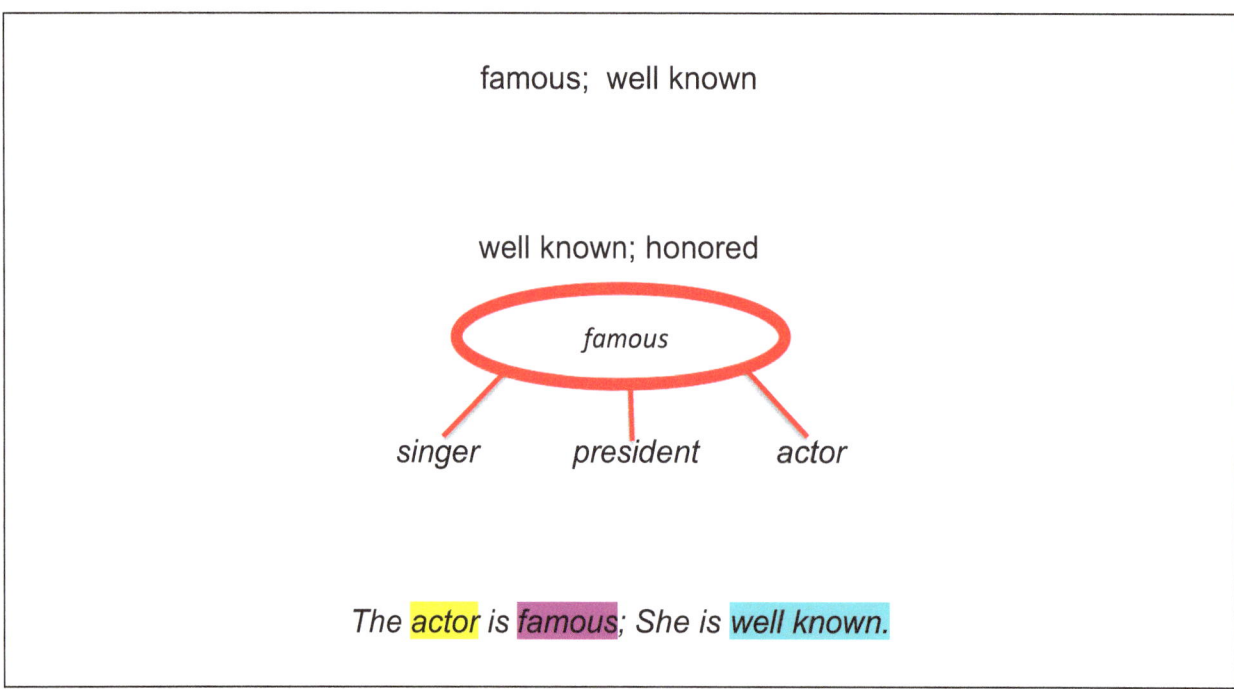

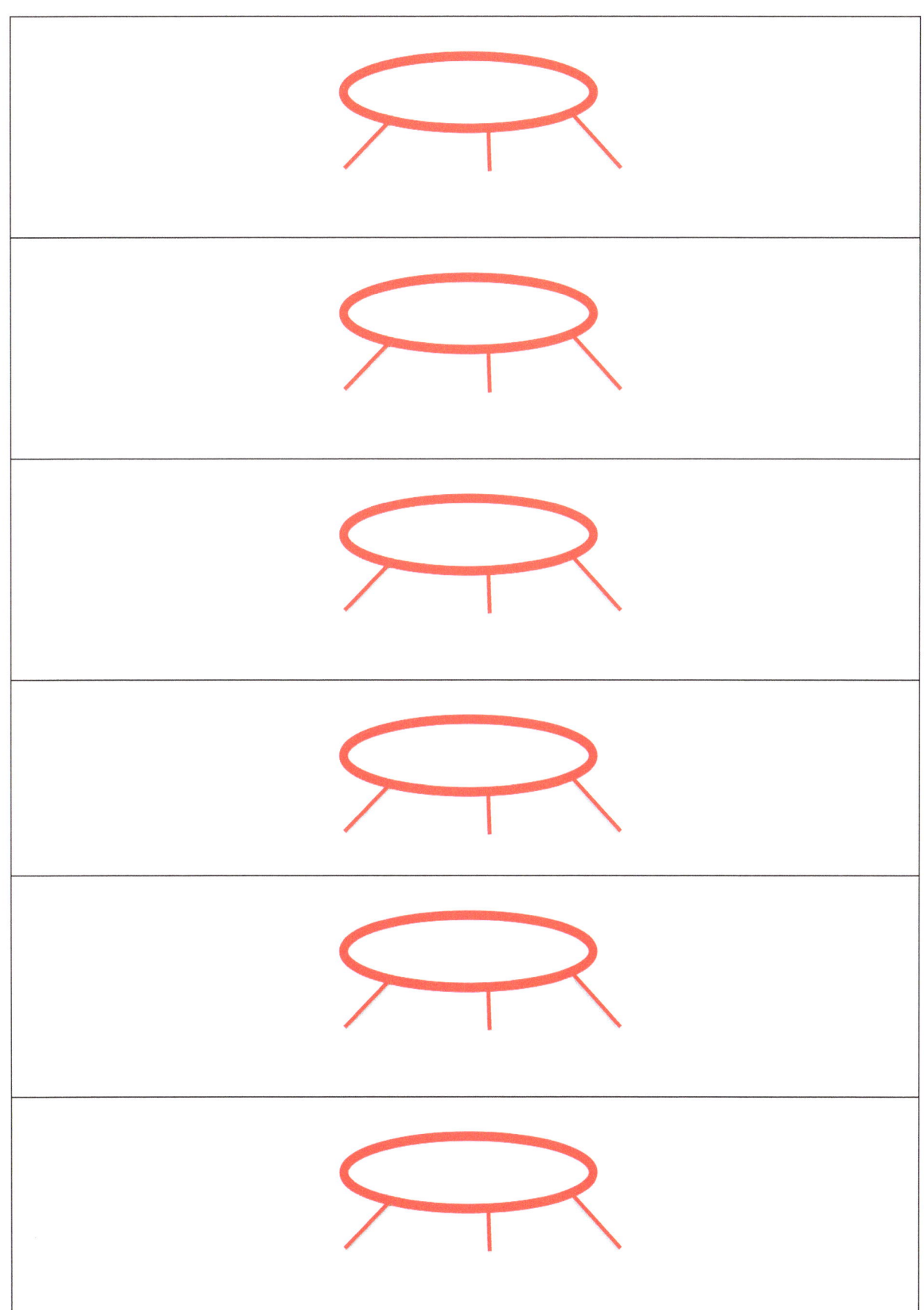

L11 Review A

Place in alphabetical order.

1. **desert**
2. **tire**
3. **famous**
4. **break**
5. **divide**
6. **whole**

L11 Review B

Unscramble the words

1. iter - _____
2. hwole - _____
3. tereds - _____
4. erbka - _____
5. uomfsa - _____
6. dvdeii - _____

L11 Test

1. _____ - to come apart; to separate into pieces

2. _____ - a dry wasteland

3. _____ - separate; split

4. whole - _____

5. tire - _____

6. famous -_____

Lesson 12

1. **humorous** - funny ; amusing

2. **pair** - a set of two; two that go together

3. **disagree** - to differ in opinion; to oppose

4. **subject** - a topic

5. **rash** - a sore on the skin

6. **doubt** - to be unsure; to question to disbelieve

L12 MEANINGFUL SENTENCES

Make a word web and write a meaningful sentence for each word in this lesson. Never try to write a meaningful sentence without first creating a word web. The word web is a part of the process for helping you transfer your new knowledge into your long-term memory. This page is your rough draft of the assignment. On a piece of notebook paper, number one-ten and rewrite each meaningful sentence. Highlight the vocabulary word pink, the context clue yellow and the definition blue. You will turn the final draft in for grading.

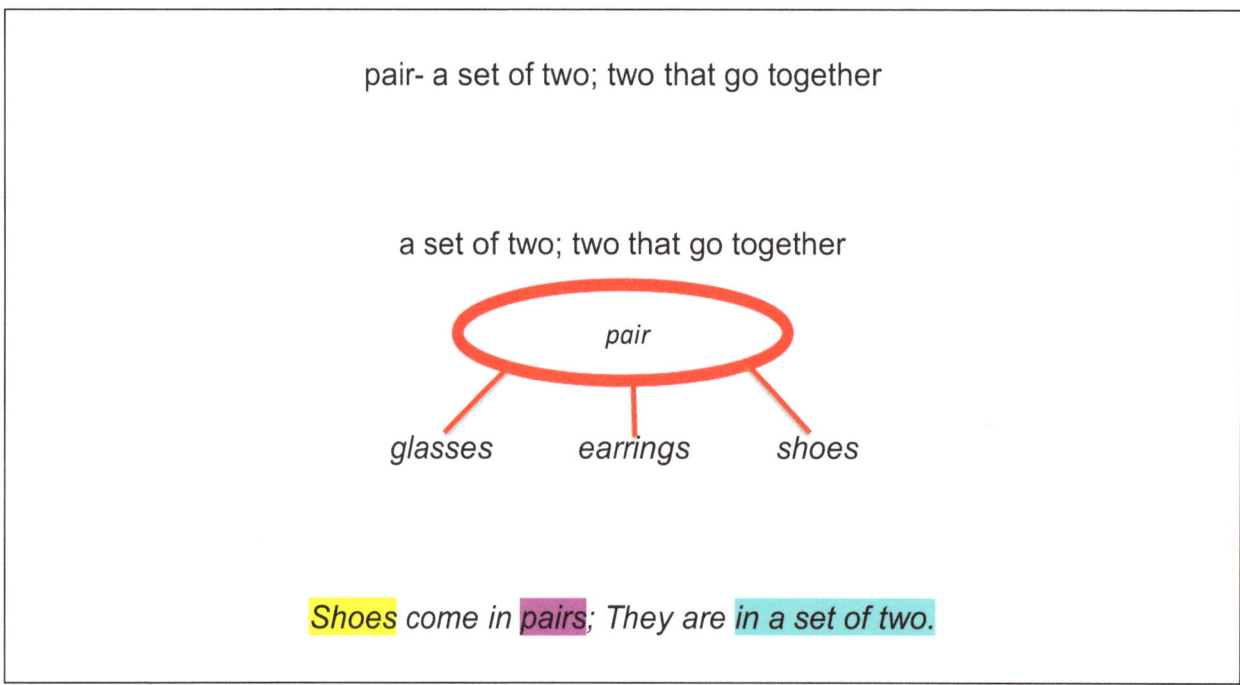

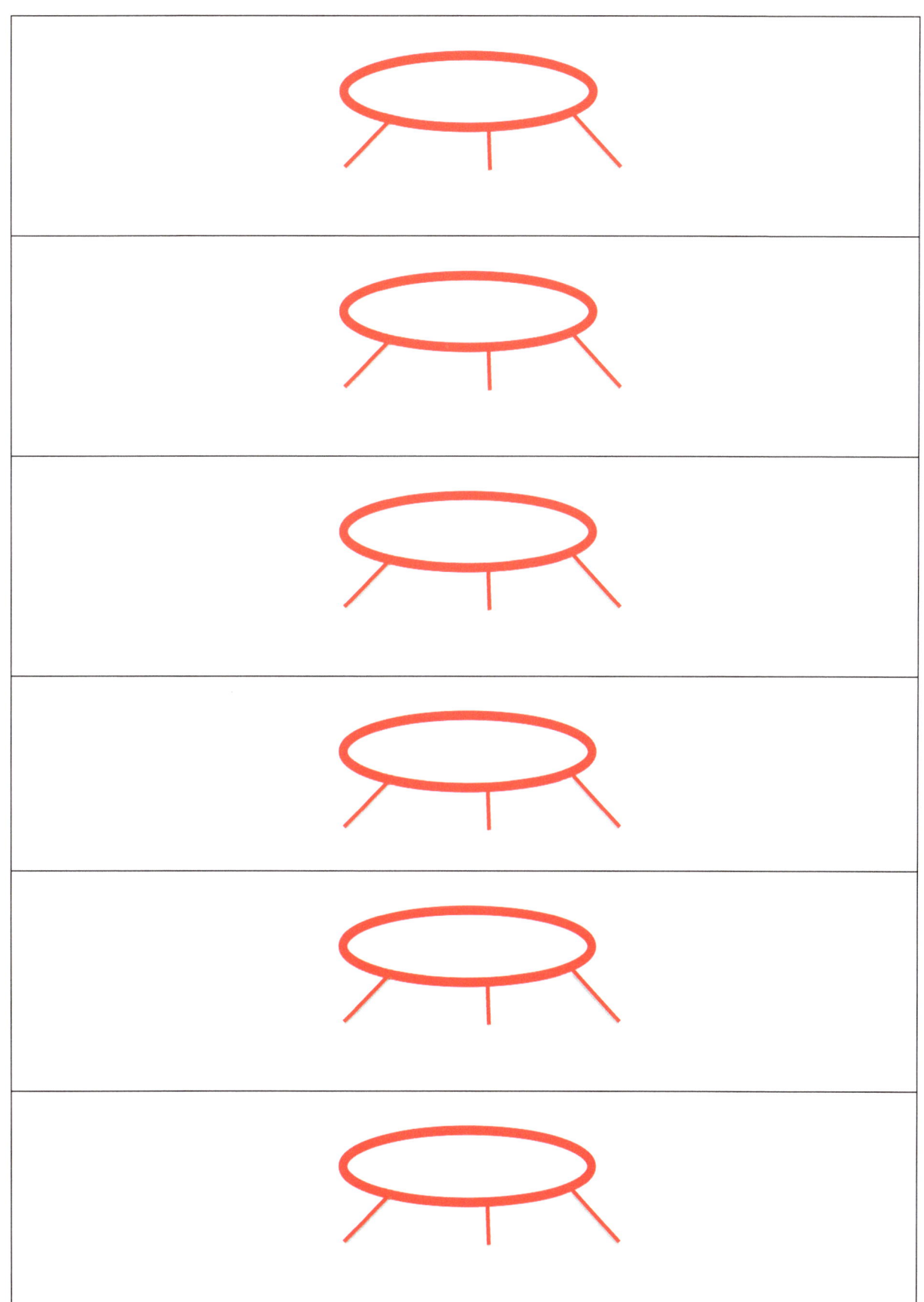

L12 Review A

Place in alphabetical order.

1. **humorous**

2. **pair**

3. **disagree**

4. **subject**

5. **rash**

6. **doubt**

L12 Review B

Unscramble the words

1. reegisda - _____

2. obudt - _____

3. pari - _____

4. btejcsu - _____

5. ahsr - _____

6. horuuoms - _____

L12 Test

1. _____ - to be unsure ; to question to disbelieve

2. _____ - funny ; amusing

3. _____ - a topic

4. rash - _____

5. pair - _____

6. disagree - _____

Lesson 13

1. **kindness** - friendly or helpful behavior; goodness
2. **outstanding** - noteworthy; famous; important
3. **ballet** - a formal dance with graceful movements
4. **learn** - to gain knowledge or skill
5. **renew** - to make new again; to restore
6. **dense** - crowded together ; thick

L13 MEANINGFUL SENTENCES

Make a word web and write a meaningful sentence for each word in this lesson. Never try to write a meaningful sentence without first creating a word web. The word web is a part of the process for helping you transfer your new knowledge into your long-term memory. This page is your rough draft of the assignment. On a piece of notebook paper, number one-ten and rewrite each meaningful sentence. Highlight the vocabulary word pink, the context clue yellow and the definition blue. You will turn the final draft in for grading.

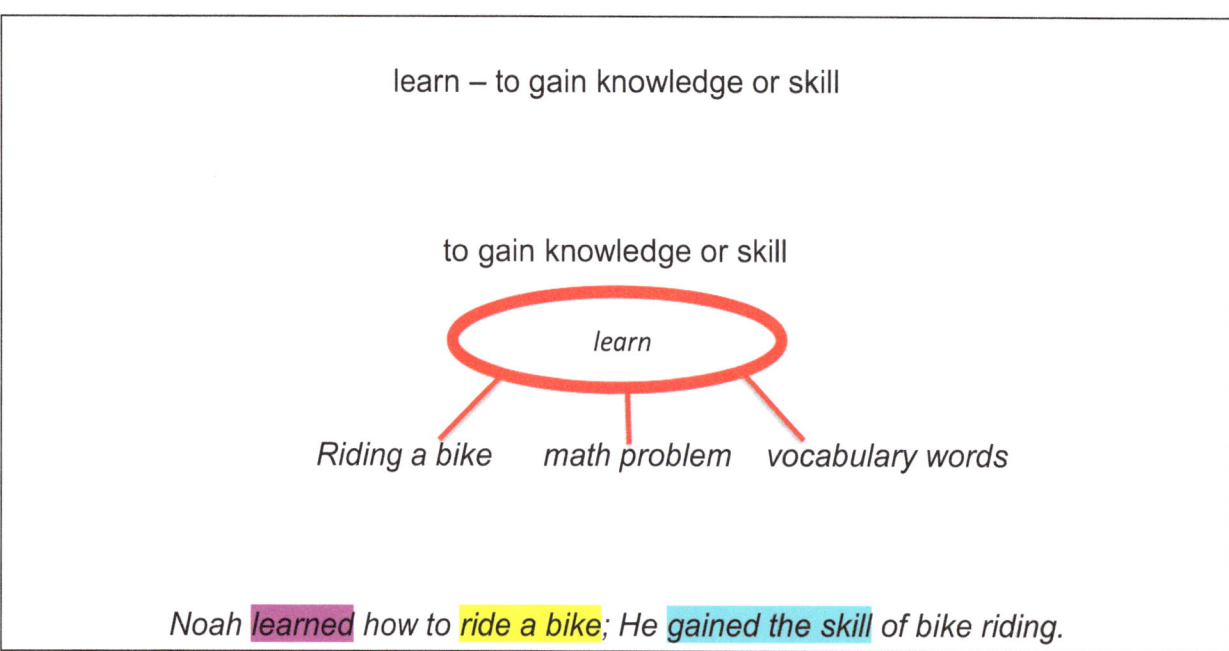

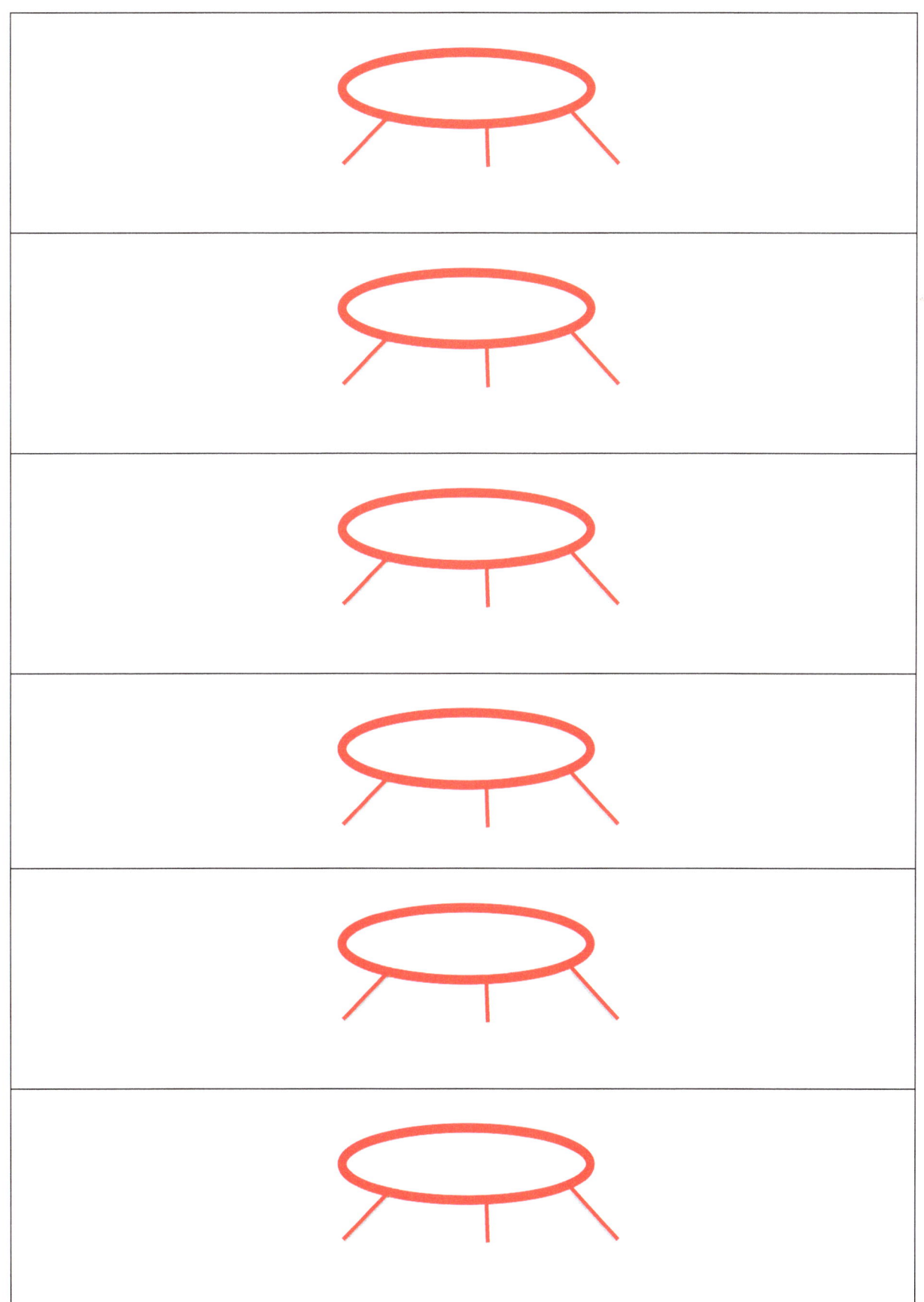

L13 Review A

Place in alphabetical order.

1. **kindness**
2. **outstanding**
3. **ballet**
4. **learn**
5. **renew**
6. **dense**

L13 Review B

Unscramble the words.

1. narel - _____
2. enwre - _____
3. ltlabe - _____
4. nksnides - _____
5. gnoiatudstn - _____
6. dsene - _____

L13 Test

1. _____ - to gain knowledge or skill

2. _____ - noteworthy; famous; important

3. _____ - a formal dance with graceful movements

4. renew - _____

5. dense - _____

6. kindness - _____

Lesson 14

1. **peaceful** - calm ; quiet; liking peace

2. **teacher** - one who provides knowledge to others; instructor; educator

3. **towering** - very high; lofty; imposing

4. **remarkable** - noteworthy; outstanding ; very special

5. **slight** - small; minor; slender

6. **entire** - whole; complete

L14 MEANINGFUL SENTENCES

Make a word web and write a meaningful sentence for each word in this lesson. Never try to write a meaningful sentence without first creating a word web. The word web is a part of the process for helping you transfer your new knowledge into your long-term memory. This page is your rough draft of the assignment. On a piece of notebook paper, number one-ten and rewrite each meaningful sentence. Highlight the vocabulary word pink, the context clue yellow and the definition blue. You will turn the final draft in for grading.

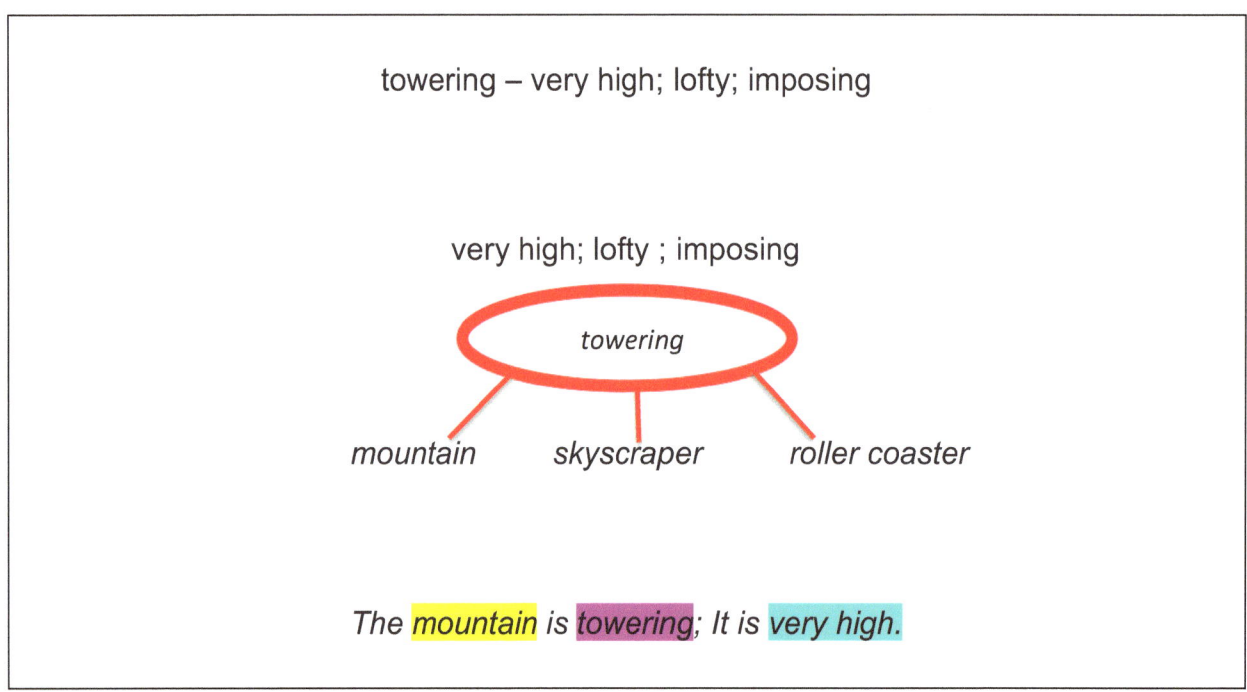

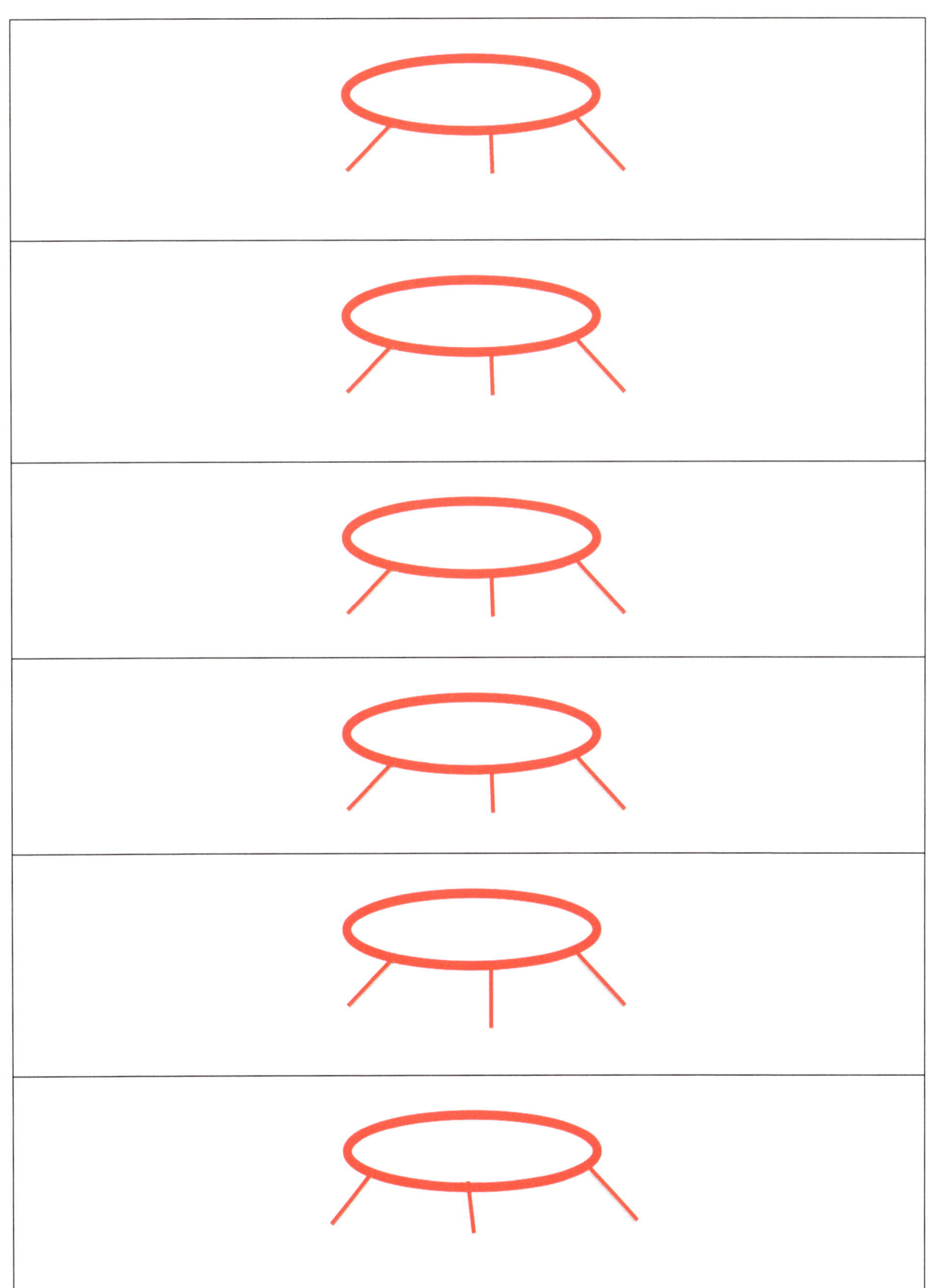

L14 Review A

Place in alphabetical order.

1. **peaceful**
2. **teacher**
3. **towering**
4. **remarkable**
5. **slight**
6. **entire**

L14 Review B

Unscramble the words.

1. bekmlerraa - _____
2. nierte - _____
3. rwiotneg - _____
4. cupelfae - _____
5. ehrtaec - _____
6. sltgih - _____

L14 Test

1. _____ - calm ; quiet; liking peace

2. _____ - one who provides knowledge to others; instructor; educator

3. _____ - very high; lofty; imposing

4. remarkable - _____

5. slight - _____

6. entire - _____

Lesson 15

1. **telephone** - a device for speaking over long distance
2. **steal** - to rob
3. **further** - to a greater extent; more
4. **aquarium** - a tank for fish
5. **liberty** - freedom; independence
6. **command** - to give an order

L15 MEANINGFUL SENTENCES

Make a word web and write a meaningful sentence for each word in this lesson. Never try to write a meaningful sentence without first creating a word web. The word web is a part of the process for helping you transfer your new knowledge into your long-term memory. This page is your rough draft of the assignment. On a piece of notebook paper, number one-ten and rewrite each meaningful sentence. Highlight the vocabulary word pink, the context clue yellow and the definition blue. You will turn the final draft in for grading.

debris; scattered pieces of waste or remains.

scattered pieces of waste or remains

debris

ashes from fire   nut shells   tree limbs from a storm

Nutshell debris littered the floor; There were scattered pieces of nut remains everywhere.

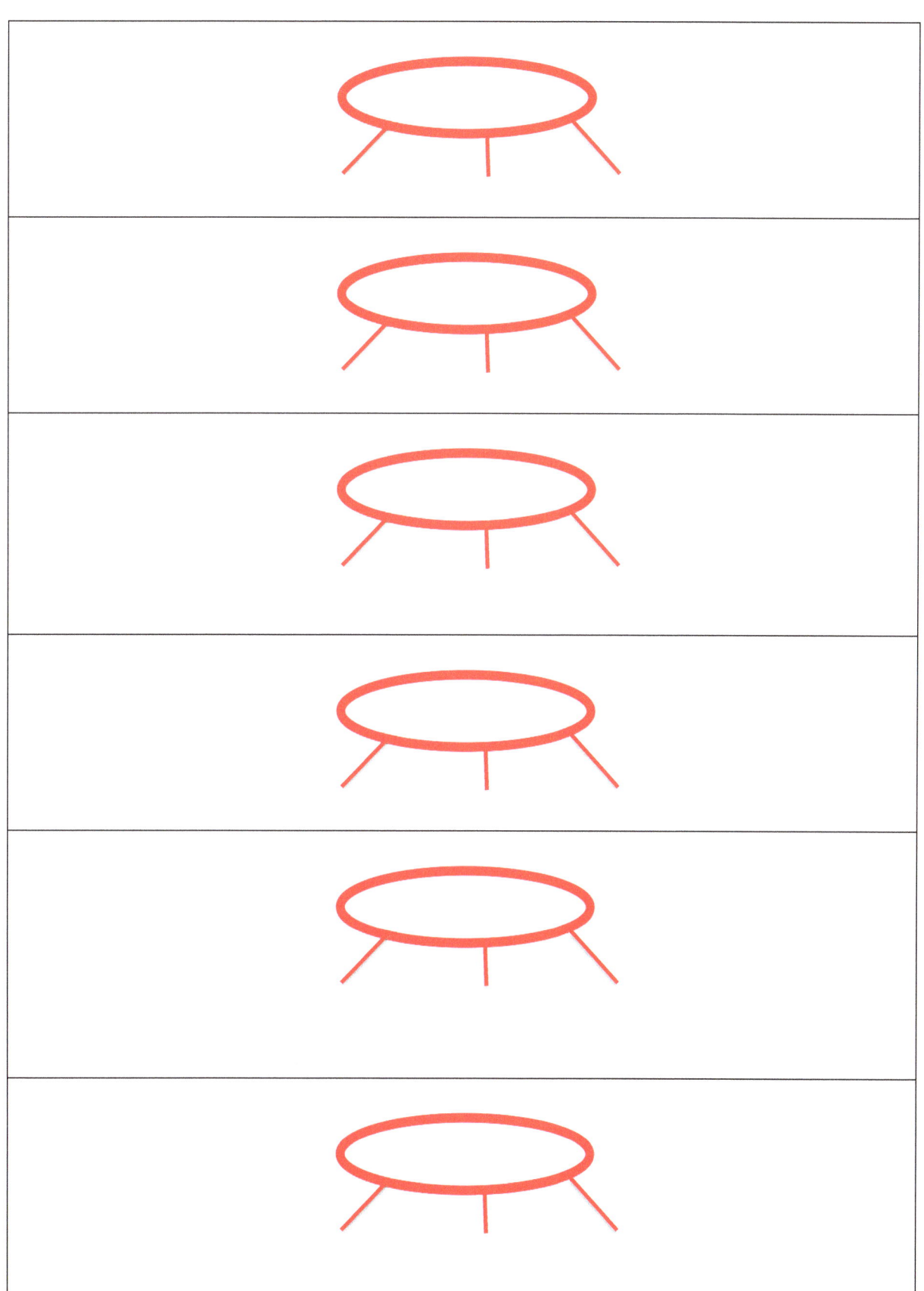

L15 Review A

Place in alphabetical order.

1. **telephone**
2. **steal**
3. **further**
4. **aquarium**
5. **liberty**
6. **command**

L15 Review B

Unscramble the words.

1. ltyirbe - _____

2. tneeopelh - _____

3. dmmcnao - _____

4. amuuraiq - _____

5. stlae - _____

6. rruethf - _____

L15 Test

1. _____ - to rob

2. _____ - a tank for fish

3. _____ - to a greater extent; more

4. command - _____

5. liberty - _____

6. telephone - _____

Lesson 16

1. **adopt** - to take into one's family by choice
2. **thoughtful** - engaged in thinking; serious; being considerate of others
3. **precaution** - an action taken in advance, usually for safety; a safeguard
4. **misplace** - to put in a wrong place; to lose
5. **exquisite** - beautifully made; very lovely; delicate
6. **dislike** - to have a bad feeling for; to object to; to disapprove

L16 MEANINGFUL SENTENCES

Make a word web and write a meaningful sentence for each word in this lesson. Never try to write a meaningful sentence without first creating a word web. The word web is a part of the process for helping you transfer your new knowledge into your long-term memory. This page is your rough draft of the assignment. On a piece of notebook paper, number one-ten and rewrite each meaningful sentence. Highlight the vocabulary word pink, the context clue yellow and the definition blue. You will turn the final draft in for grading.

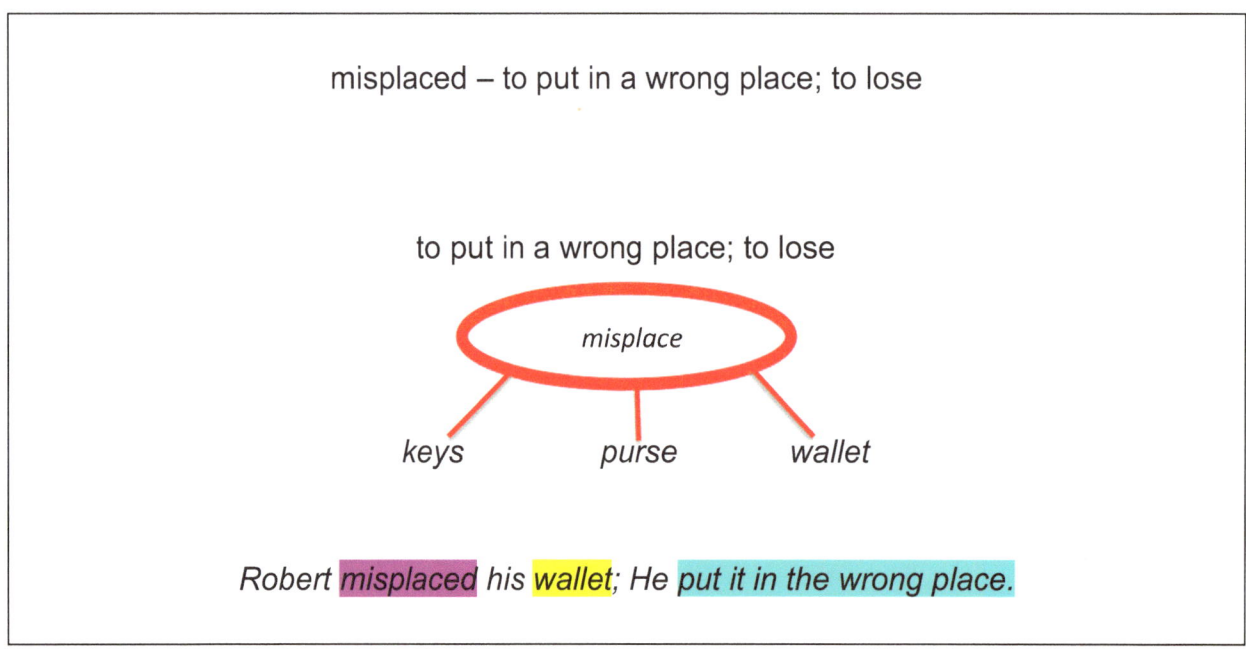

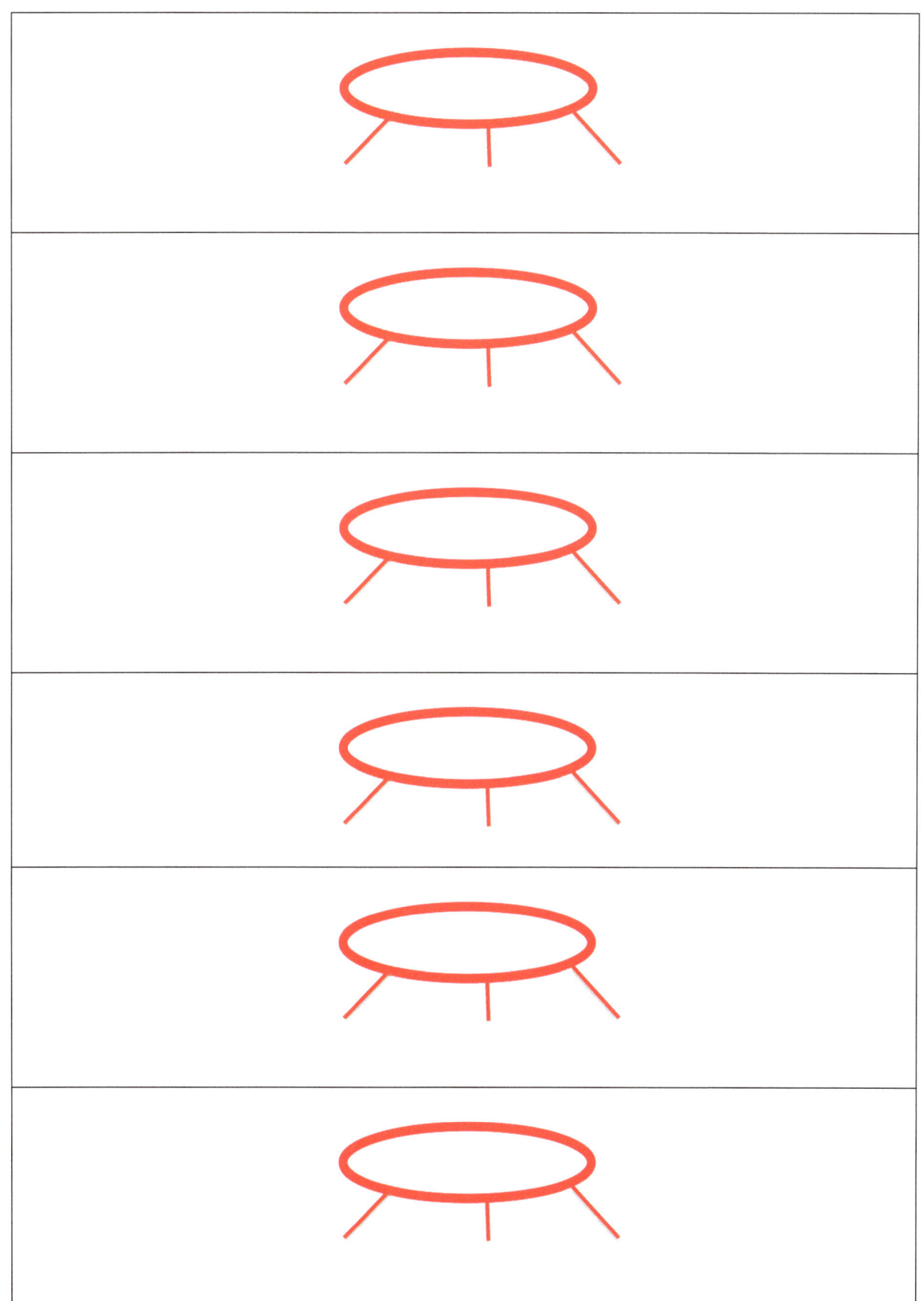

L16 Review A

Place in alphabetical order.

1. **adopt**
2. **thoughtful**
3. **precaution**
4. **misplace**
5. **exquisite**
6. **dislike**

L16 Review B

Unscramble the words

1. iediskl - _____
2. gluhfhtout - _____
3. xteqsieui - _____
4. adtop - _____
5. spileacm - _____
6. necaitorpu - _____

L16 Test

1. _____ - beautifully made; very lovely; delicate

2. _____ - to put in a wrong place; to lose

3. _____ - an action taken in advance, usually for safety; a safeguard

4. adopt - _____

5. dislike - _____

6. thoughtful - _____

Lesson 17

1. **comical** - funny; amusing

2. **autograph** - a person's signature

3. **descent** - the act of coming down

4. **cute** - pretty; attractive

5. **desert** - dry, barren land

6. **agreement** - an understanding or arrangement between people

L17 MEANINGFUL SENTENCES

Make a word web and write a meaningful sentence for each word in this lesson. Never try to write a meaningful sentence without first creating a word web. The word web is a part of the process for helping you transfer your new knowledge into your long-term memory. This page is your rough draft of the assignment. On a piece of notebook paper, number one-ten and rewrite each meaningful sentence. Highlight the vocabulary word pink, the context clue yellow and the definition blue. You will turn the final draft in for grading.

autograph – a person's signature

a person's signature

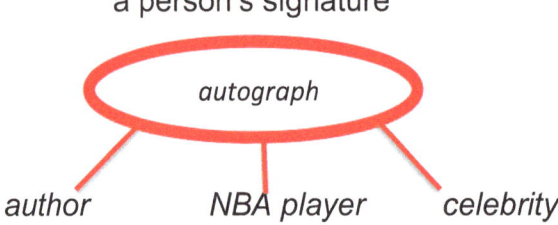

author   NBA player   celebrity

Everyone was lined up to get an autograph *from the* celebrity*; They wanted his* signature.

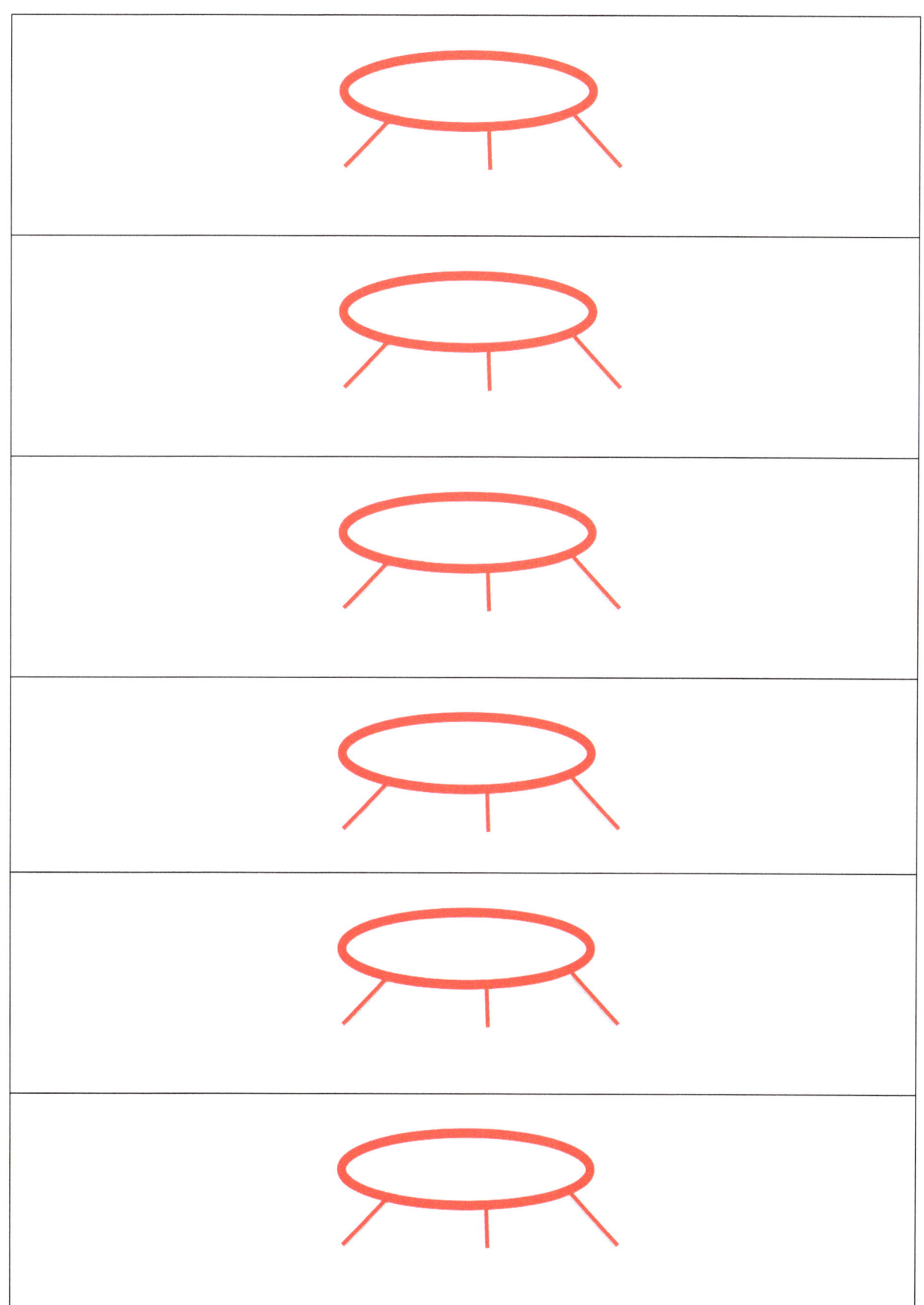

L17 Review A

Place in alphabetical order.

1. **comical**
2. **autograph**
3. **descent**
4. **cute**
5. **desert**
6. **agreement**

L17 Review B

Unscramble the words.

1. setder - _____

2. mocalic - _____

3. tmegenaer - _____

4. ucte - _____

5. tenedcs - _____

6. toguaprah - _____

L17 Test

1. _____ - a person's signature

2. _____ - funny; amusing

3. _____ - an understanding or arrangement between people

4. cute - _____

5. desert - _____

6. descent - _____

Lesson 18

1. **wind** - moving air
2. **school** - a place for learning
3. **gather** -to bring together
4. **hear** - to listen
5. **meet** - to come together; to encounter
6. **argue** -to disagree; to quarrel; to dispute

L18 MEANINGFUL SENTENCES

Make a word web and write a meaningful sentence for each word in this lesson. Never try to write a meaningful sentence without first creating a word web. The word web is a part of the process for helping you transfer your new knowledge into your long-term memory. This page is your rough draft of the assignment. On a piece of notebook paper, number one-ten and rewrite each meaningful sentence. Highlight the vocabulary word pink, the context clue yellow and the definition blue. You will turn the final draft in for grading.

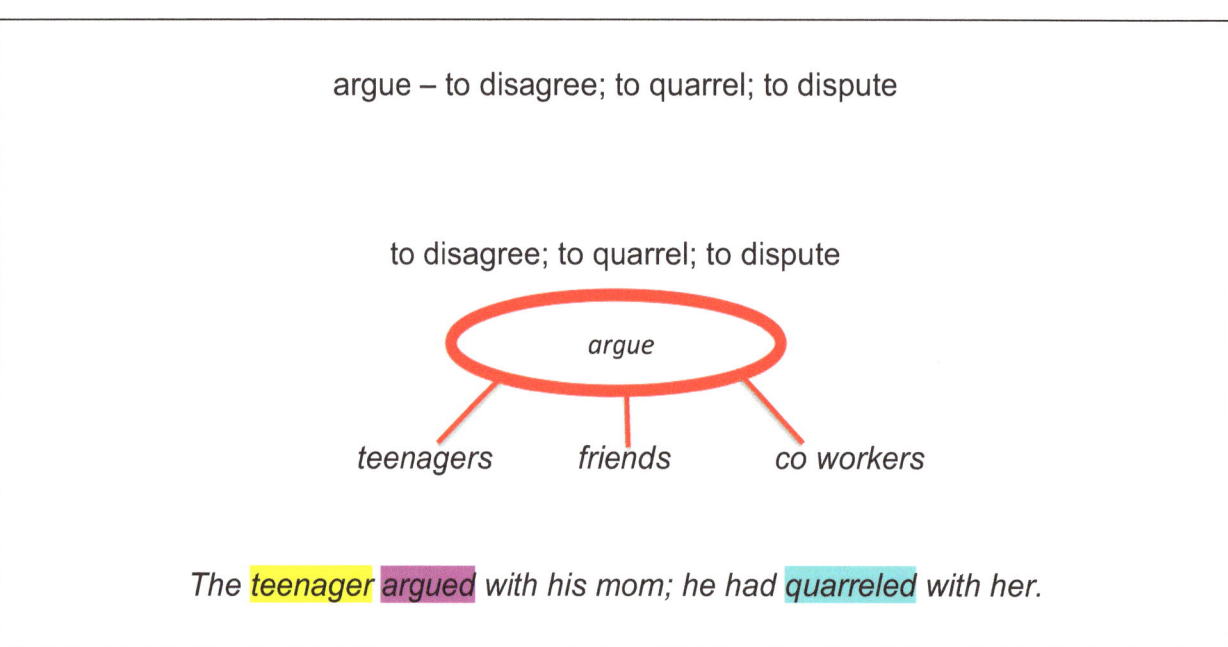

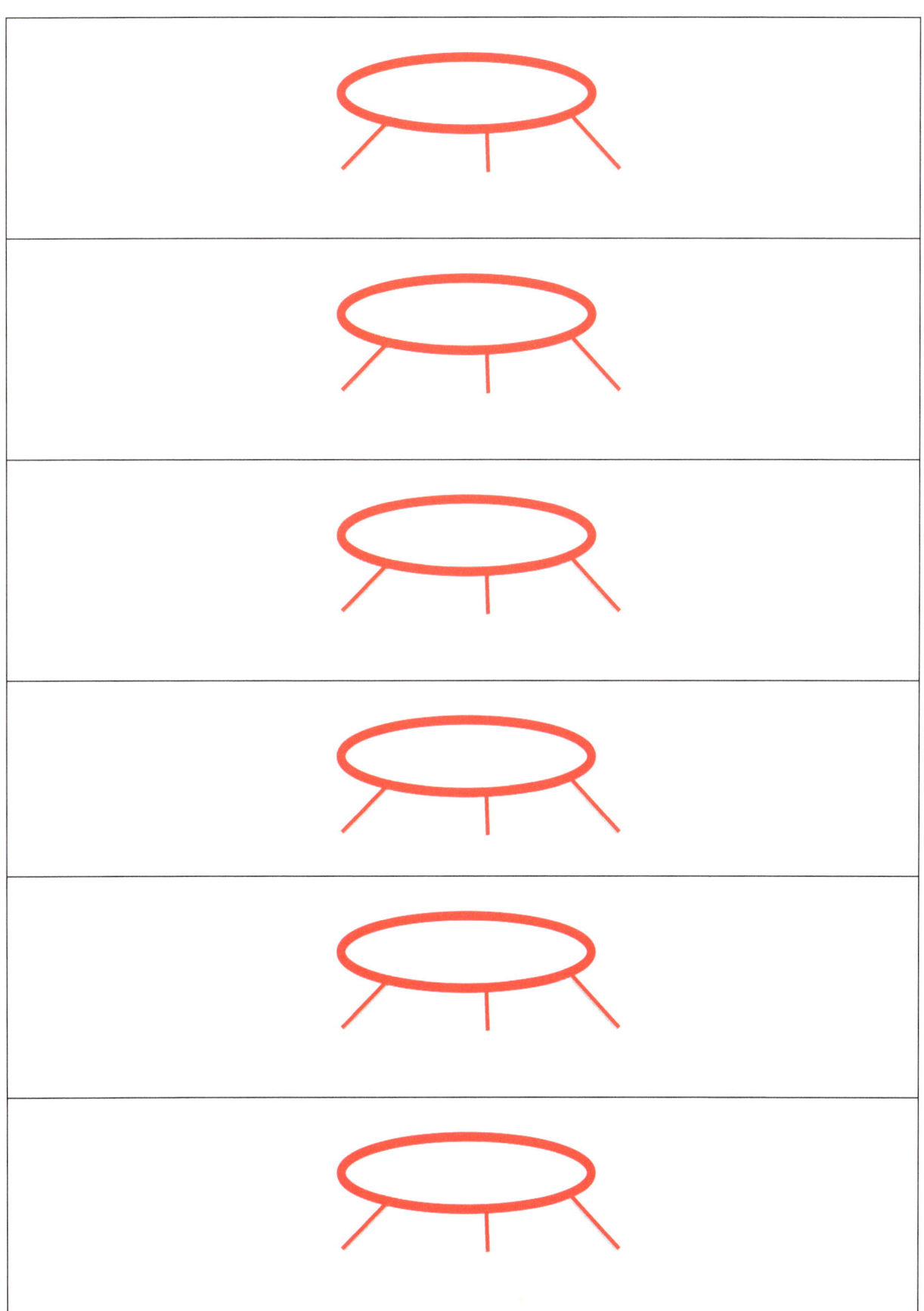

18 Review A

Place in alphabetical order.

1. **wind**
2. **school**
3. **gather**
4. **hear**
5. **meet**
6. **argue**

L18 Review B

Unscramble the words.

1. hare - _____
2. gurea - _____
3. etem - _____
4. indw - _____
5. tgrahe - _____
6. sohcol - _____

L18 Test

1. _____ - a place for learning

2. _____ -to disagree; to quarrel; to dispute

3. _____ - to come together; to encounter

4. gather -_____

5. wind - _____

6. hear - _____

TRIMESTER 2 EXAM

1. tire - _____
2. loose - _____
3. meet - _____
4. autograph - _____
5. apology - _____
6. disagree - _____
7. entire - _____
8. aquarium - _____
9. famous - _____
10. towering - _____
11. liberty - _____
12. whole - _____
13. comical - _____
14. slight - _____
15. yard - _____
16. school - _____
17. aquatic - _____
18. outstanding - _____
19. rash - _____
20. pair - _____
21. command - _____
22. remarkable - _____
23. ballet - _____
24. kindness - _____

25. steal - _____

26. gather - _____

27. misplace - _____

28. descent - _____

29. divide - _____

30. doubt - _____

31. break - _____

32. argue - _____

33. hear - _____

34. further - _____

35. dislike - _____

36. teacher - _____

37. peaceful - _____

38. exquisite - _____

39. humorous - _____

40. desert - _____

41. adopt - _____

42. dense - _____

43. learn - _____

44. cute - _____

45. quit - _____

46. subject - _____

47. wind - _____

48. matriarch - _____

49. renew - _____

50. desert - _____

Lesson 19

1. **narrow** - not wide; thin

2. **excessive** - extreme; too much

3. **campus** - the grounds of a school or college

4. **cyclone** - a powerful storm; tornado

5. **loyalty** - devotion; faithfulness

6. **great** -very big in size or number

L19 MEANINGFUL SENTENCES

Make a word web and write a meaningful sentence for each word in this lesson. Never try to write a meaningful sentence without first creating a word web. The word web is a part of the process for helping you transfer your new knowledge into your long-term memory. This page is your rough draft of the assignment. On a piece of notebook paper, number one-ten and rewrite each meaningful sentence. Highlight the vocabulary word pink, the context clue yellow and the definition blue. You will turn the final draft in for grading.

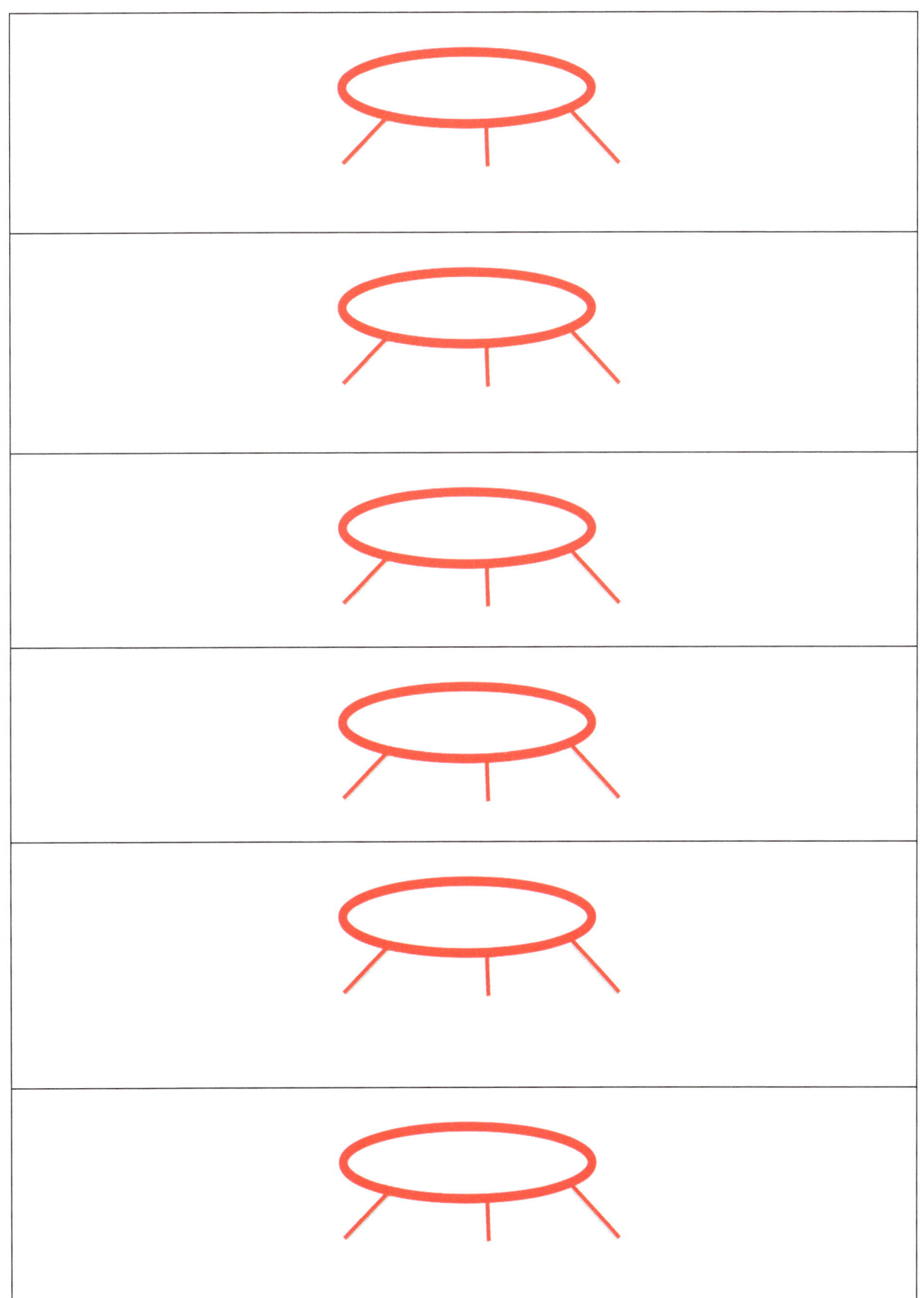

L19 Review A

Place in alphabetical order.

1. **narrow**
2. **excessive**
3. **campus**
4. **cyclone**
5. **loyalty**
6. **great**

L19 Review B

Unscramble the words.

1. cvsesieex - _____
2. scaupm - _____
3. oranrw - _____
4. eragt - _____
5. yotlaly - _____
6. celoycn - _____

L19 Test

1. _____ - a powerful storm; tornado

2. _____ - not wide; thin

3. _____ - devotion; faithfulness

4. great - _____

5. excessive - _____

6. campus - _____

Lesson 20

1. **powerful** -strong ; mighty

2. **close** - to shut

3. **grammar** - the study of the forms and uses of words in sentences

4. **later** - coming after the proper time

5. **diagram** - a drawing that shows how something works

6. **boundary** - border; edge; margin

L20 MEANINGFUL SENTENCES

Make a word web and write a meaningful sentence for each word in this lesson. Never try to write a meaningful sentence without first creating a word web. The word web is a part of the process for helping you transfer your new knowledge into your long-term memory. This page is your rough draft of the assignment. On a piece of notebook paper, number one-ten and rewrite each meaningful sentence. Highlight the vocabulary word pink, the context clue yellow and the definition blue. You will turn the final draft in for grading.

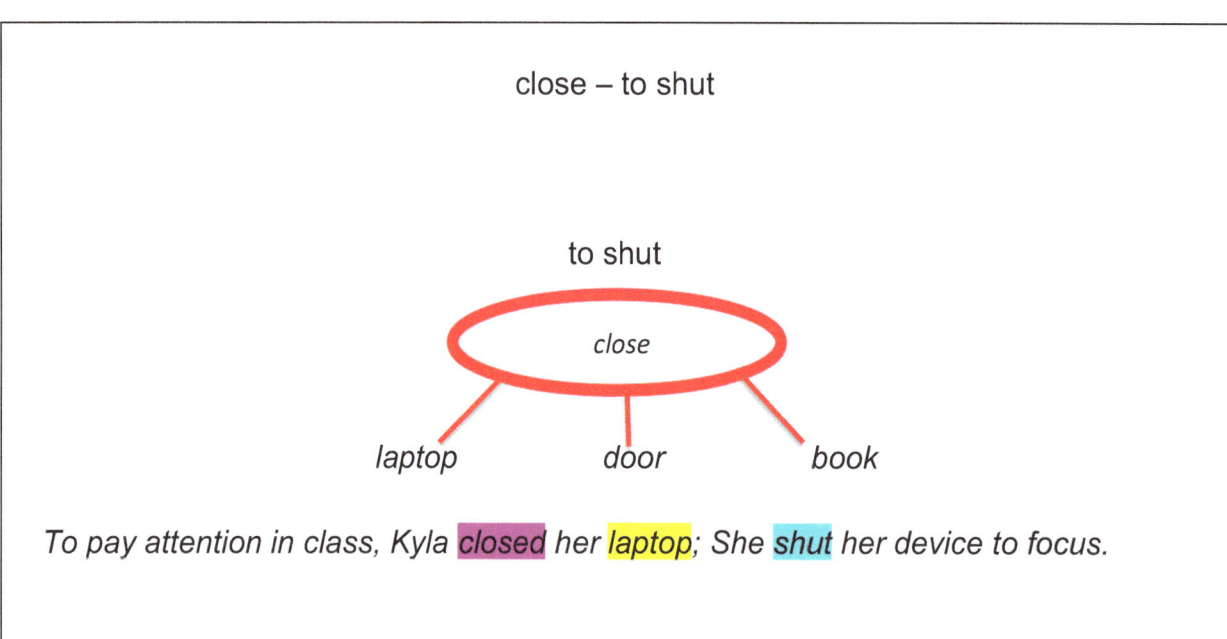

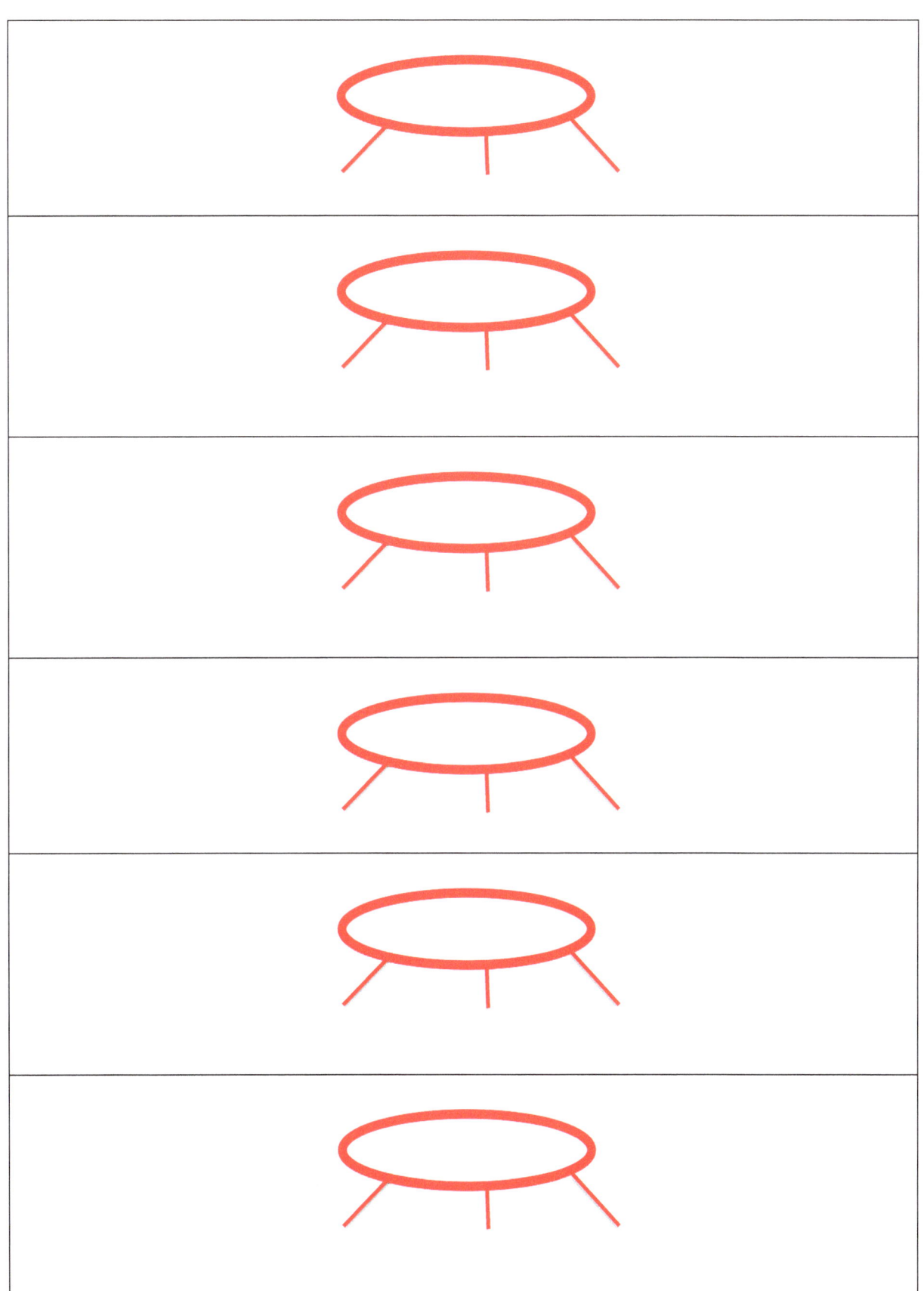

L20 Review A

Place in alphabetical order.

1. **powerful**
2. **close**
3. **grammar**
4. **later**
5. **diagram**
6. **boundary**

L20 Review B

Unscramble the words

1. plrufwoe - _____
2. ecsol - _____
3. gaammrr - _____
4. talre - _____
5. miadagr - _____
6. ubrndoay - _____

L20 Test

1. _____ - the study of the forms and uses of words in sentences

2. _____ - strong ; mighty

3. _____ - a drawing that shows how something works

4. close - _____

5. boundary - _____

6. later - _____

Lesson 21

1. **rewrite** - to write again, especially to improve writing; to revise

2. **conflict** -struggle; battle; fight; war

3. **quiet** - silent; having little noise; calm

4. **root** - to cheer for a person or team

5. **resent** - to feel offended

6. **contain** - to have; to hold ; to include

L21 MEANINGFUL SENTENCES

Make a word web and write a meaningful sentence for each word in this lesson. Never try to write a meaningful sentence without first creating a word web. The word web is a part of the process for helping you transfer your new knowledge into your long-term memory. This page is your rough draft of the assignment. On a piece of notebook paper, number one-ten and rewrite each meaningful sentence. Highlight the vocabulary word pink, the context clue yellow and the definition blue. You will turn the final draft in for grading.

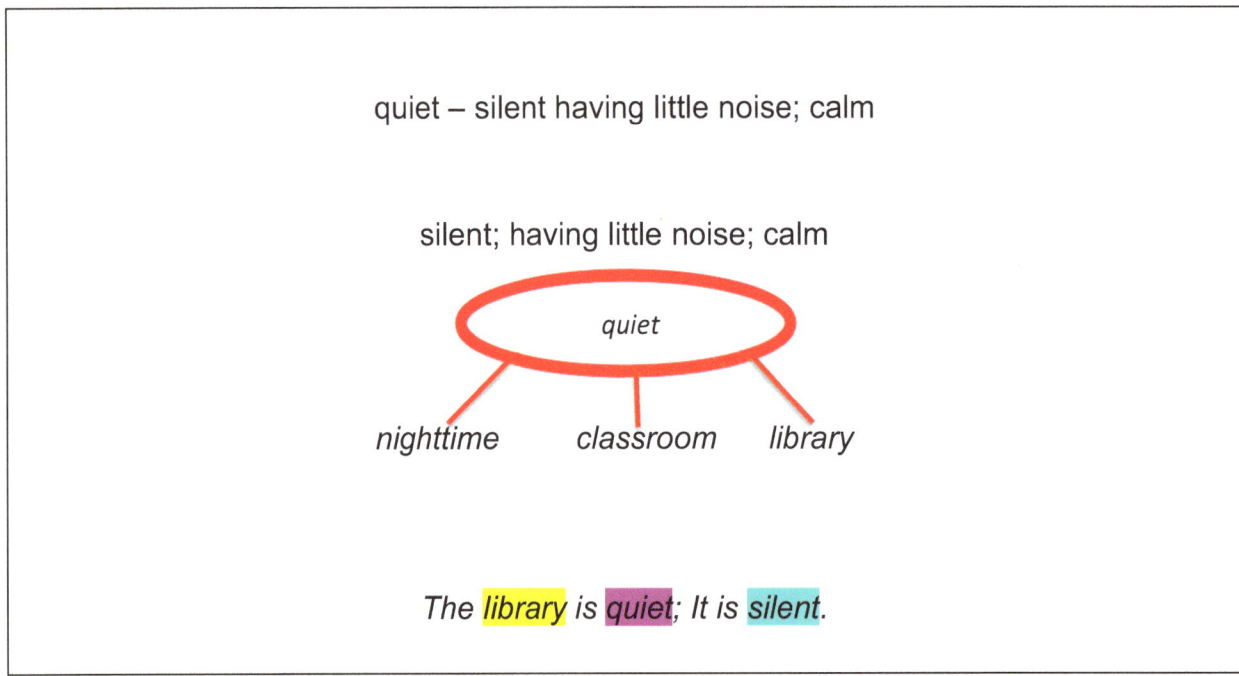

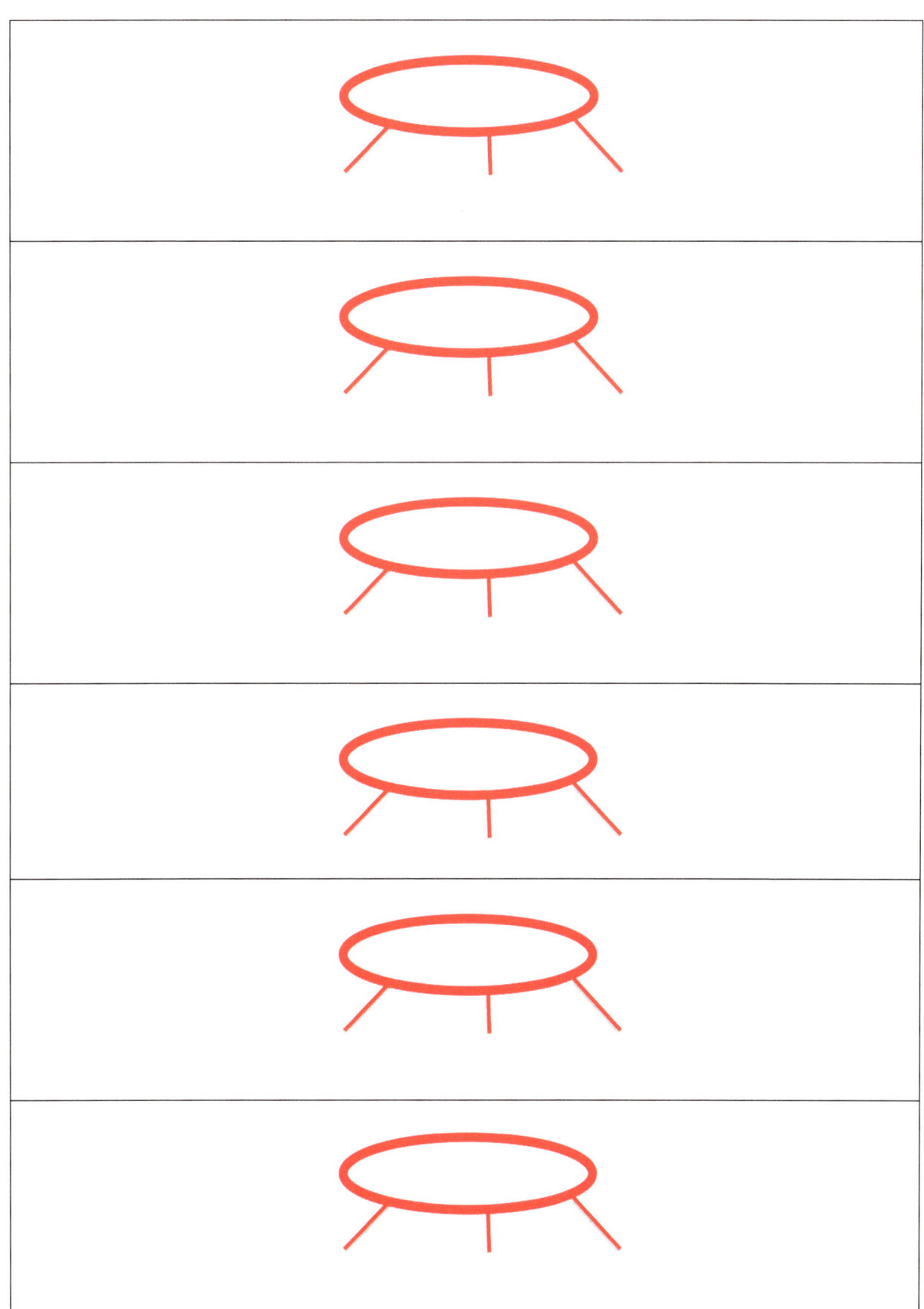

L21 Review A

Place in alphabetical order.

1. **rewrite**
2. **conflict**
3. **quiet**
4. **root**
5. **resent**
6. **contain**

L21 Review B

Unscramble the words

1. rnetse - _____
2. toro - _____
3. ctcfniol - _____
4. ireerwt - _____
5. eitqu - _____
6. ticnoan - _____

L21 Test

1. _____ -struggle; battle; fight; war

2. _____ - to cheer for a person or team

3. _____ - to write again, especially to improve writing; to revise

4. quiet - _____

5. resent - _____

6. contain - _____

Lesson 22

1. **waste** -to make poor use of; to spend foolishly

2. **unsure** - not certain; doubtful

3. **dishonest** - untrustworthy; deceitful

4. **popular** - well liked

5. **ball** - a formal dance

6. **tiny** -small; little

L22 MEANINGFUL SENTENCES

Make a word web and write a meaningful sentence for each word in this lesson. Never try to write a meaningful sentence without first creating a word web. The word web is a part of the process for helping you transfer your new knowledge into your long-term memory. This page is your rough draft of the assignment. On a piece of notebook paper, number one-ten and rewrite each meaningful sentence. Highlight the vocabulary word pink, the context clue yellow and the definition blue. You will turn the final draft in for grading.

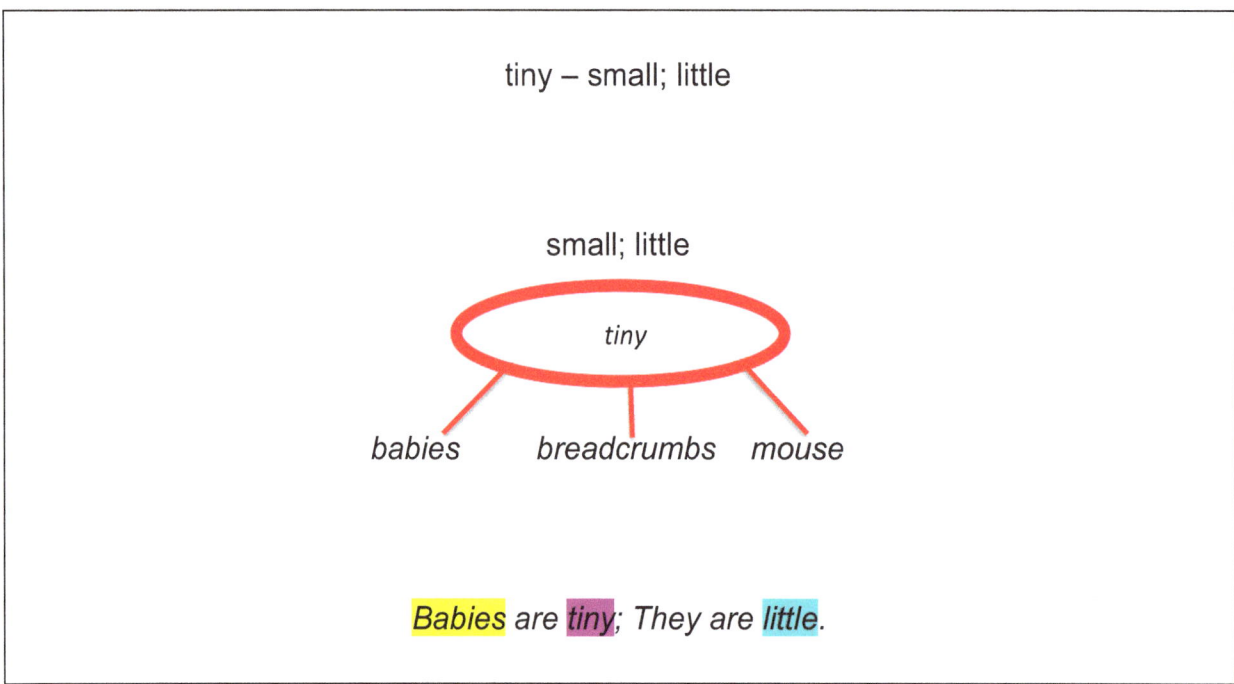

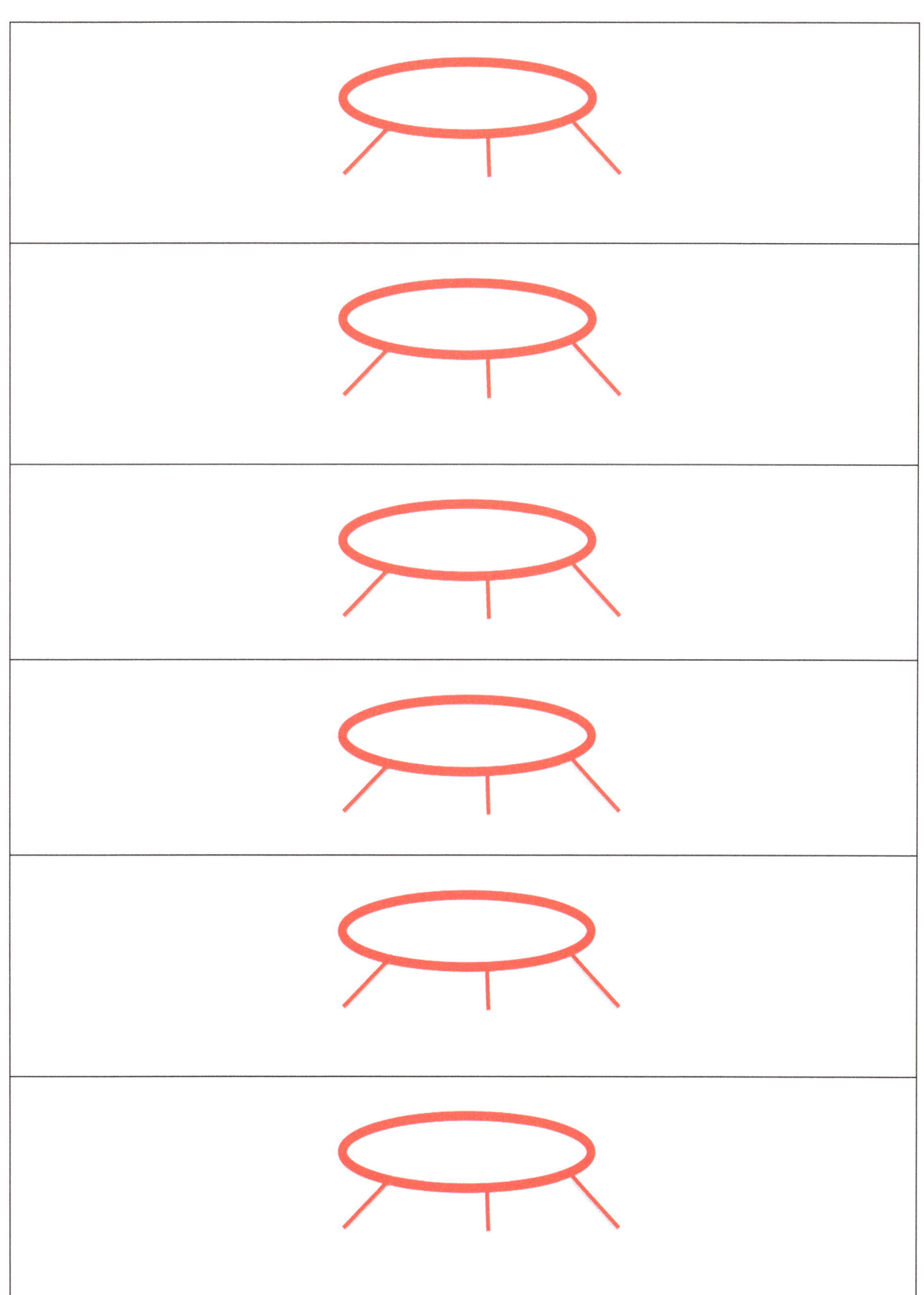

L22 Review A

Place in alphabetical order.

1. waste
2. unsure
3. dishonest
4. popular
5. ball
6. tiny

L22 Review B

Unscramble the words.

1. setaw - _____
2. urunse - _____
3. odthesins - _____
4. ruppalo - _____
5. llba - _____
6. tiyn - _____

L22 Test

1. _____ - not certain; doubtful

2. _____ - to make poor use of; to spend foolishly

3. _____ - small; little

4. popular - _____

5. dishonest - _____

6. ball - _____

Lesson 23

1. **careless** - not cautious; reckless; sloppy

2. **transport** - to carry from one place to another

3. **agree** - to consent; to accept

4. **custom** -a usual action; a long-established habit

5. **cycle** - a regularly repeated event or series of events

6. **unsafe** - dangerous; risky

L23 MEANINGFUL SENTENCES

Make a word web and write a meaningful sentence for each word in this lesson. Never try to write a meaningful sentence without first creating a word web. The word web is a part of the process for helping you transfer your new knowledge into your long-term memory. This page is your rough draft of the assignment. On a piece of notebook paper, number one-ten and rewrite each meaningful sentence. Highlight the vocabulary word pink, the context clue yellow and the definition blue. You will turn the final draft in for grading.

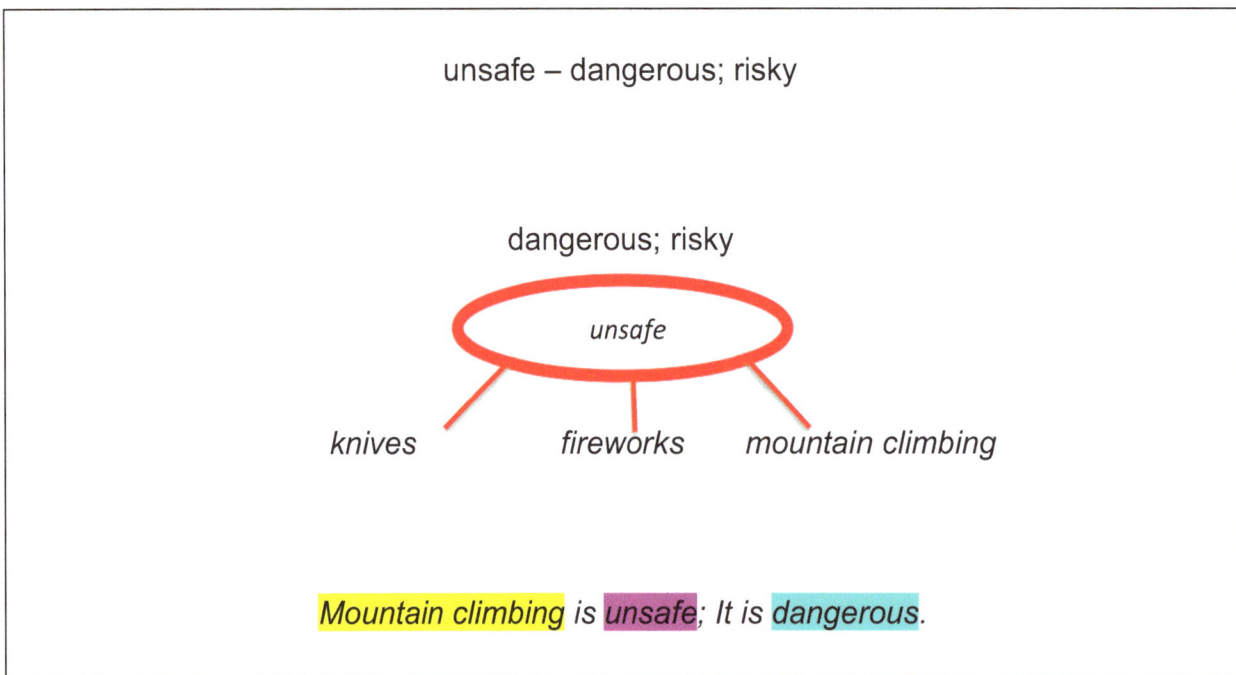

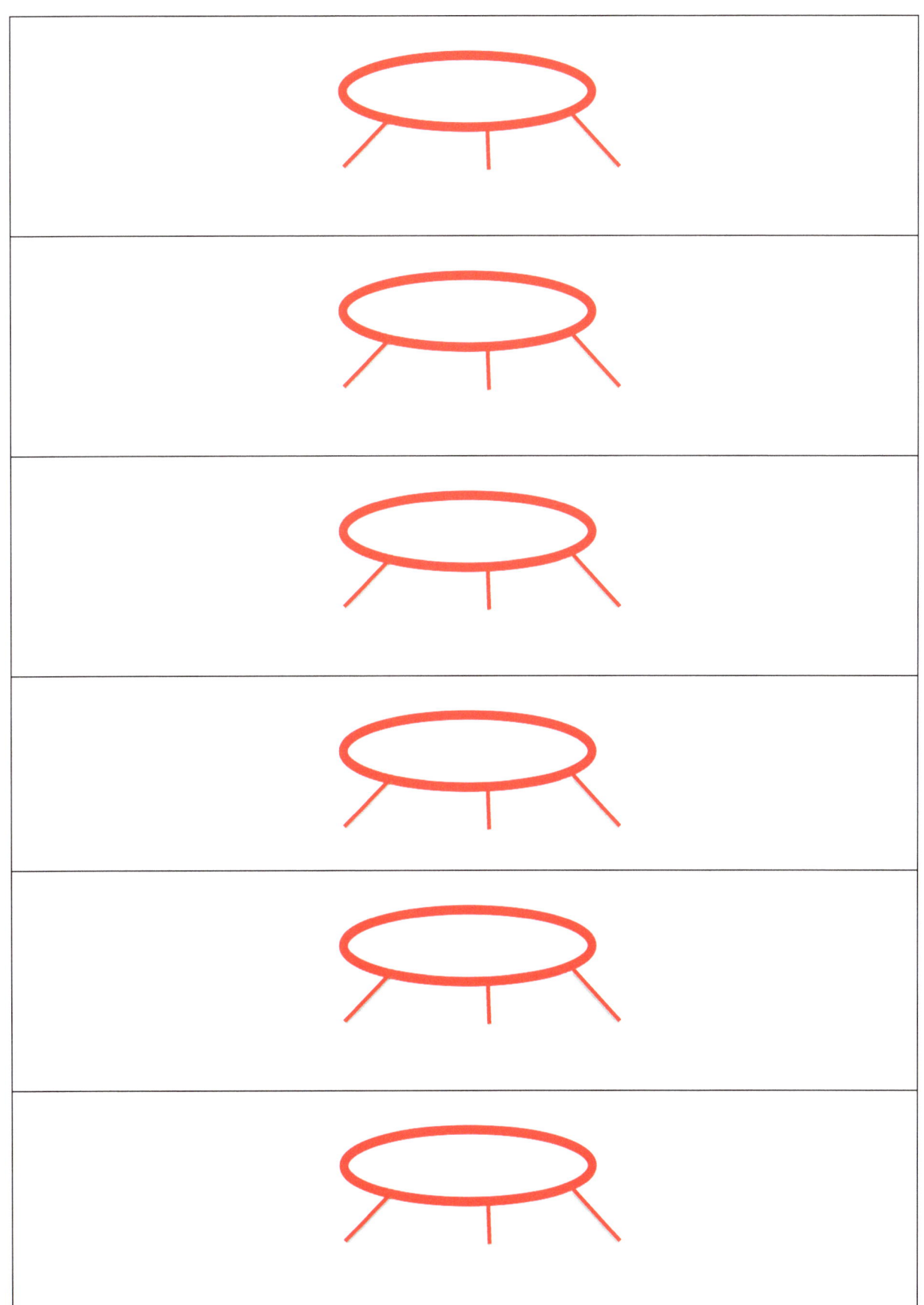

L23 Review A

Place in alphabetical order.

1. careless
2. transport
3. agree
4. custom
5. cycle
6. unsafe

L23 Review B

Unscramble the words.

1. elccy - _____
2. uesfan - _____
3. oustcm - _____
4. caessrle - _____
5. srrtonpat - _____
6. ergae - _____

L23 Test

1. _____ -a usual action; a long-established habit

2. _____ - to consent; to accept

3. _____ - a regularly repeated event or series of events

4. unsafe - _____

5. transport - _____

6. careless - _____

Lesson 24

1. **territory** - land; an area that a government exercises authority over

2. **selfish** - thinking of oneself; having no care for others

3. **action** - the process of doing something; act ; deed

4. **tear** -to pull apart; to rip into pieces

5. **government** - a system for ruling a nation, a nation, state, city, or town

6. **night** - the time between sunrise and sunset

L24 MEANINGFUL SENTENCES

Make a word web and write a meaningful sentence for each word in this lesson. Never try to write a meaningful sentence without first creating a word web. The word web is a part of the process for helping you transfer your new knowledge into your long-term memory. This page is your rough draft of the assignment. On a piece of notebook paper, number one-ten and rewrite each meaningful sentence. Highlight the vocabulary word pink, the context clue yellow and the definition blue. You will turn the final draft in for grading.

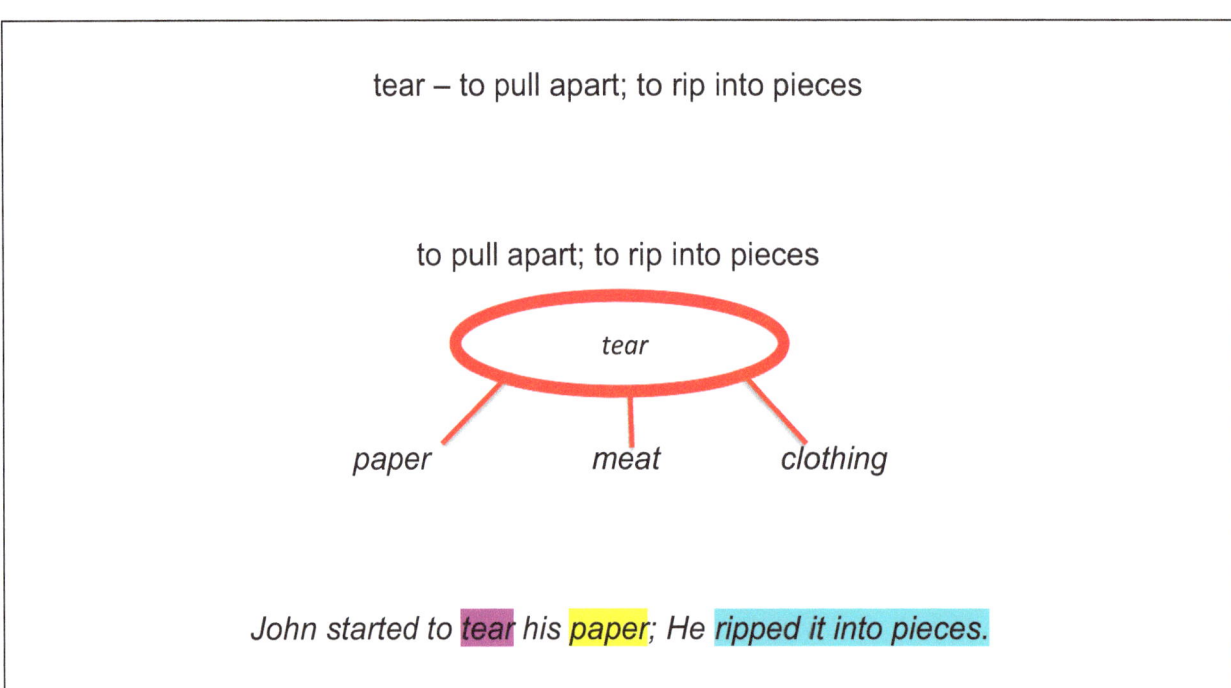

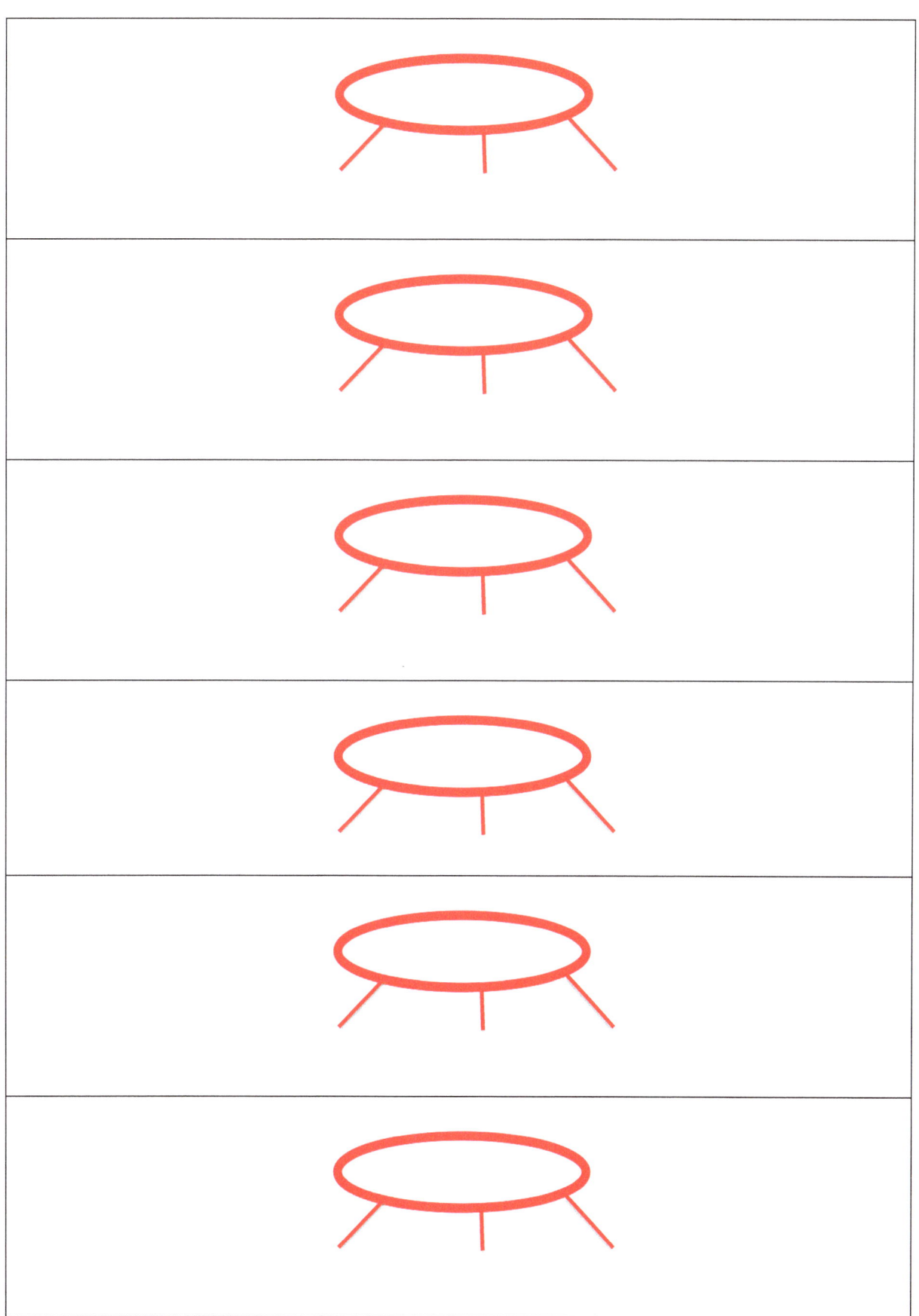

L24 Review A

Place in alphabetical order.

1. **territory**
2. **selfish**
3. **action**
4. **tear**
5. **government**
6. **night**

L24 Review B

Unscramble the words.

1. hngti - _____
2. ater - _____
3. reitytror - _____
4. ishesfl - _____
5. aiotnc - _____
6. tnovegemrn - _____

L24 Test

1. _____ - a system for ruling a nation, a nation, state, city, or town

2. _____ - the time between sunrise and sunset

3. _____ - the process of doing something; act ; deed

4. tear - _____

5. territory - _____

6. selfish - _____

Lesson 25

1. **failure** - defeat; not being successful

2. **primitive**: uncivilized; undeveloped; early ; original

3. **cheap** - inexpensive; costing little

4. **breathe** -to inhale and exhale

5. **firm** - hard; solid; steady

6. **present** - a gift

L25 MEANINGFUL SENTENCES

Make a word web and write a meaningful sentence for each word in this lesson. Never try to write a meaningful sentence without first creating a word web. The word web is a part of the process for helping you transfer your new knowledge into your long-term memory. This page is your rough draft of the assignment. On a piece of notebook paper, number one-ten and rewrite each meaningful sentence. Highlight the vocabulary word pink, the context clue yellow and the definition blue. You will turn the final draft in for grading.

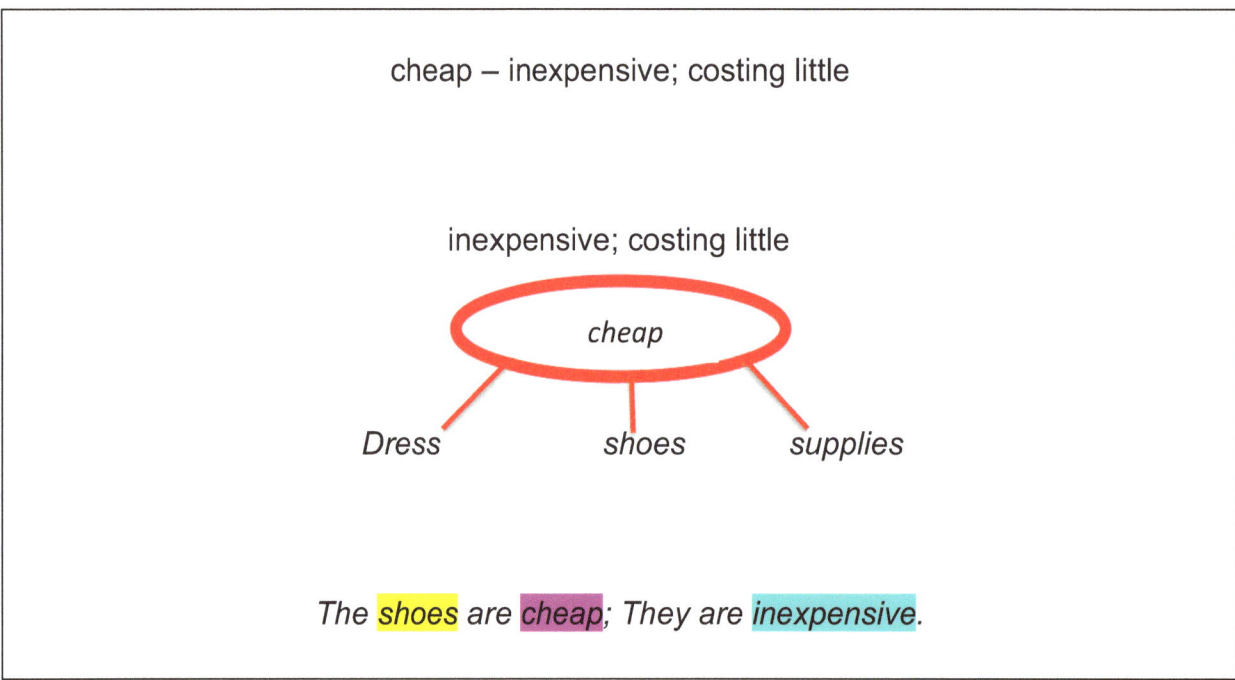

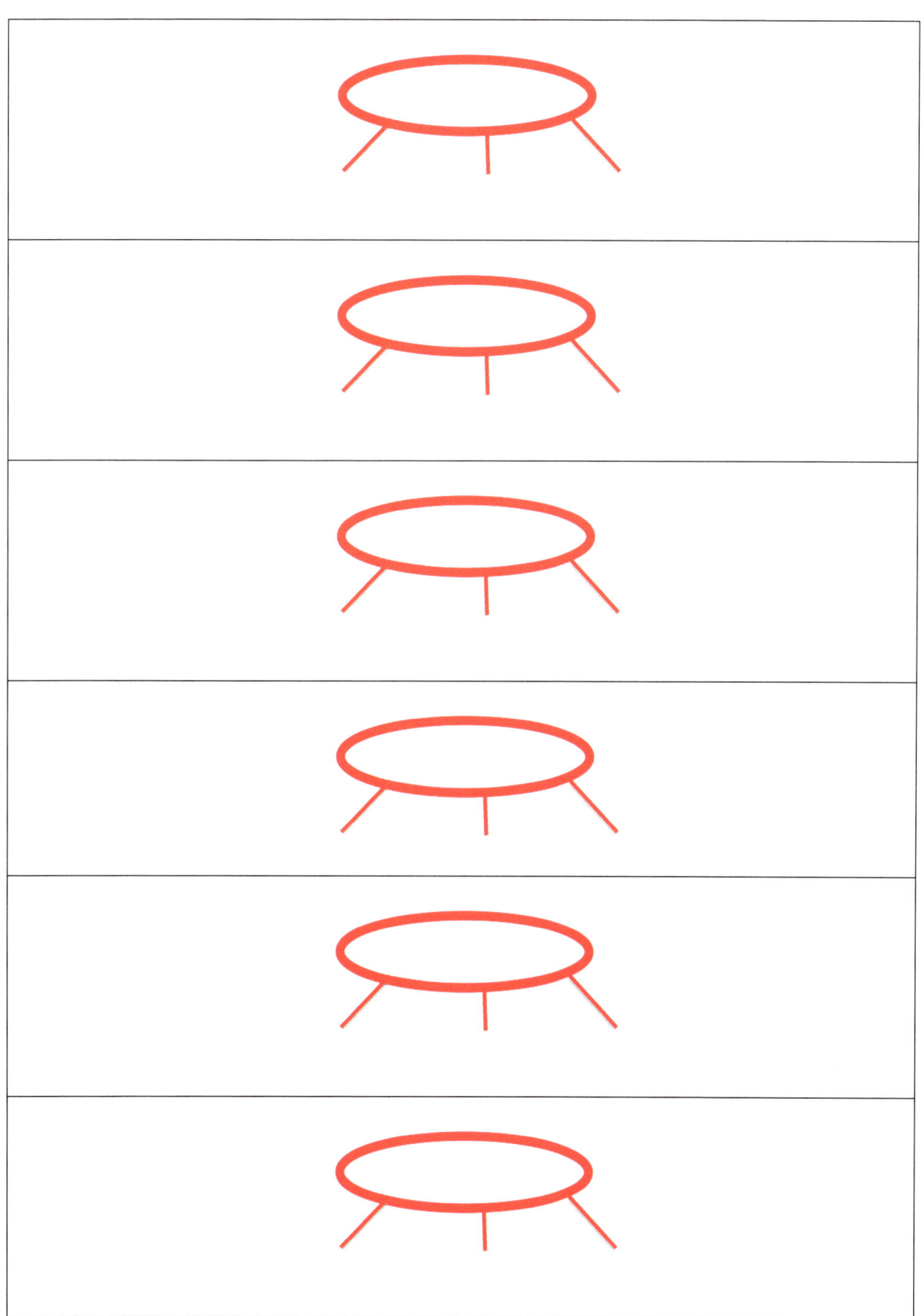

L25 Review A

Place in alphabetical order.

1. **failure**
2. **primitive**
3. **cheap**
4. **breathe**
5. **firm**
6. **present**

L25 Review B

Unscramble the words.

1. tearhbe - _____
2. paehc - _____
3. lruefai - _____
4. ifmr - _____
5. repsnet - _____
6. ripvetimi - _____

L25 Test

1. _____ - a gift

2. _____ - defeat; not being successful

3. _____ - inexpensive; costing little

4. primitive: _____

5. firm - _____

6. breathe - _____

Lesson 26

1. **right** - correct ; proper

2. **weary** - tired; exhausted; worn out

3. **barometer** - an instrument

4. **prune** - to trim

5. **advise** - to give advice

6. **except** - leaving out; not including

L26 MEANINGFUL SENTENCES

Make a word web and write a meaningful sentence for each word in this lesson. Never try to write a meaningful sentence without first creating a word web. The word web is a part of the process for helping you transfer your new knowledge into your long-term memory. This page is your rough draft of the assignment. On a piece of notebook paper, number one-ten and rewrite each meaningful sentence. Highlight the vocabulary word pink, the context clue yellow and the definition blue. You will turn the final draft in for grading.

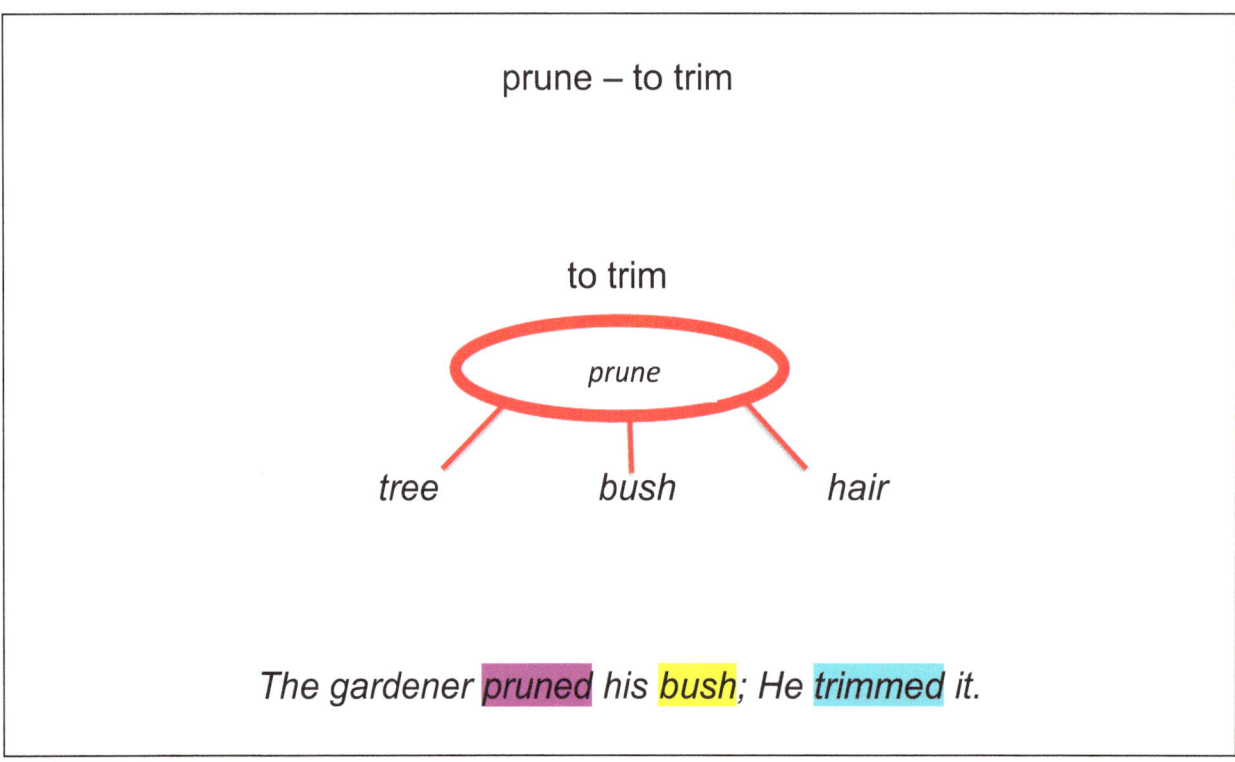

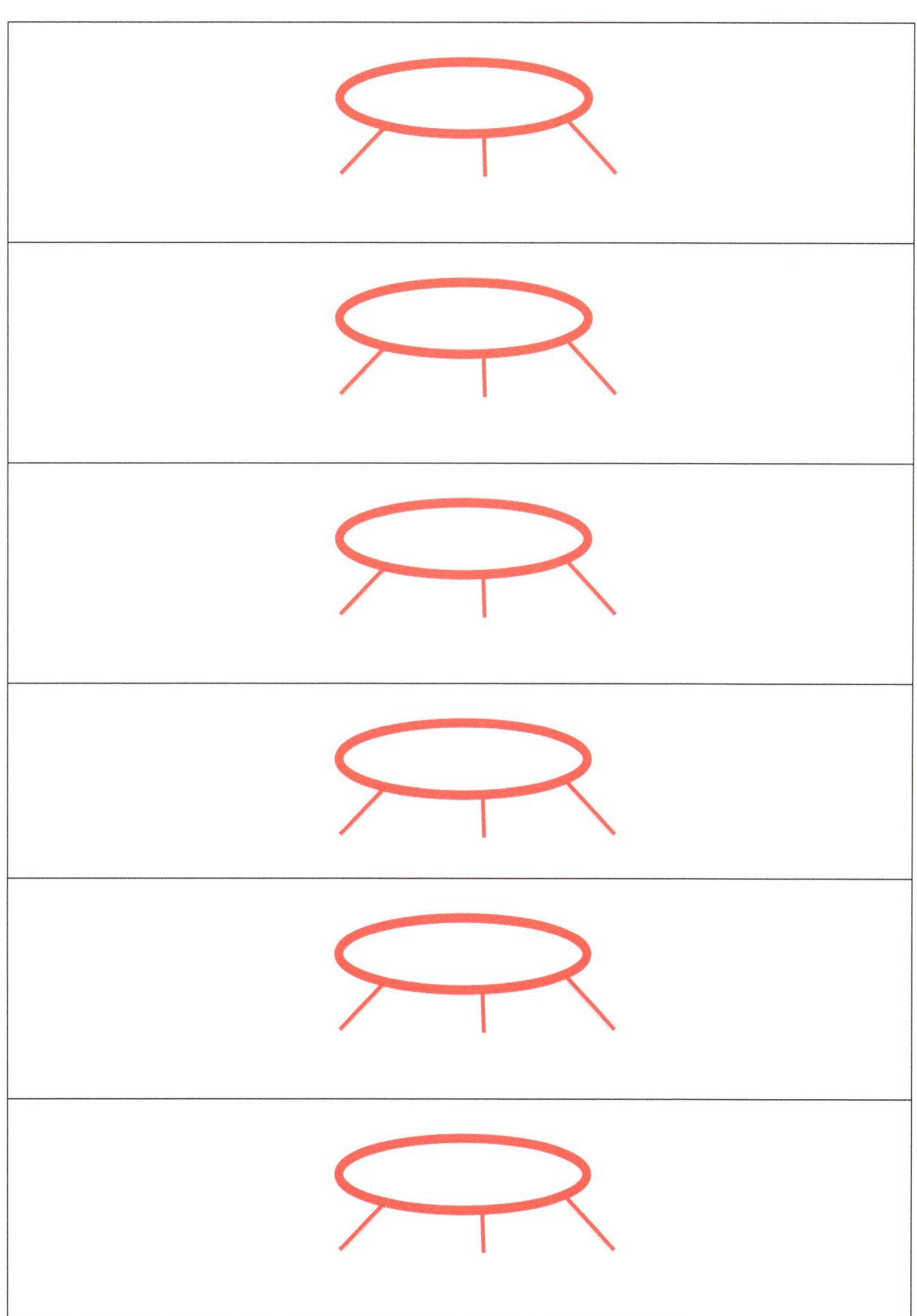

L26 Review A

Place in alphabetical order.

1. **right**
2. **weary**
3. **barometer**
4. **prune**
5. **advise**
6. **except**

L26 Review B

Unscramble the words

1. trroaemeb - _____
2. eexcpt - _____
3. ghrit - _____
4. eayrw - _____
5. seidva - _____
6. nupre - _____

L26 Test

1. _____ - leaving out; not including

2. _____ - tired; exhausted; worn out

3. _____ - to give advice

4. barometer - _____

5. prune - _____

6. right - _____

Lesson 27

1. **prologue** - an introduction or opening to a story

2. **uniform** - clothes worn by members of a group or team

3. **brave** - courageous; fearless

4. **geography** - the study of the earth's surface

5. **sadness** - sorrow; grief; unhappiness

6. **finale** – an exciting ending

L27 MEANINGFUL SENTENCES

Make a word web and write a meaningful sentence for each word in this lesson. Never try to write a meaningful sentence without first creating a word web. The word web is a part of the process for helping you transfer your new knowledge into your long-term memory. This page is your rough draft of the assignment. On a piece of notebook paper, number one-ten and rewrite each meaningful sentence. Highlight the vocabulary word pink, the context clue yellow and the definition blue. You will turn the final draft in for grading.

uniform – clothes worn by members of a group or team

scattered pieces of waste or remains

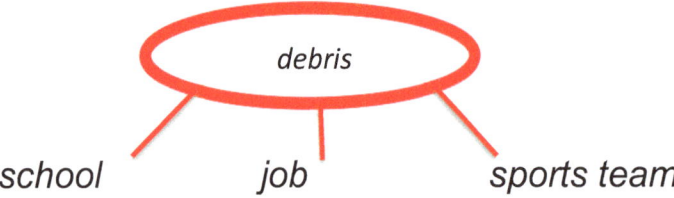

school   job   sports team

Robert has a school uniform; He has clothes for by members of the school.

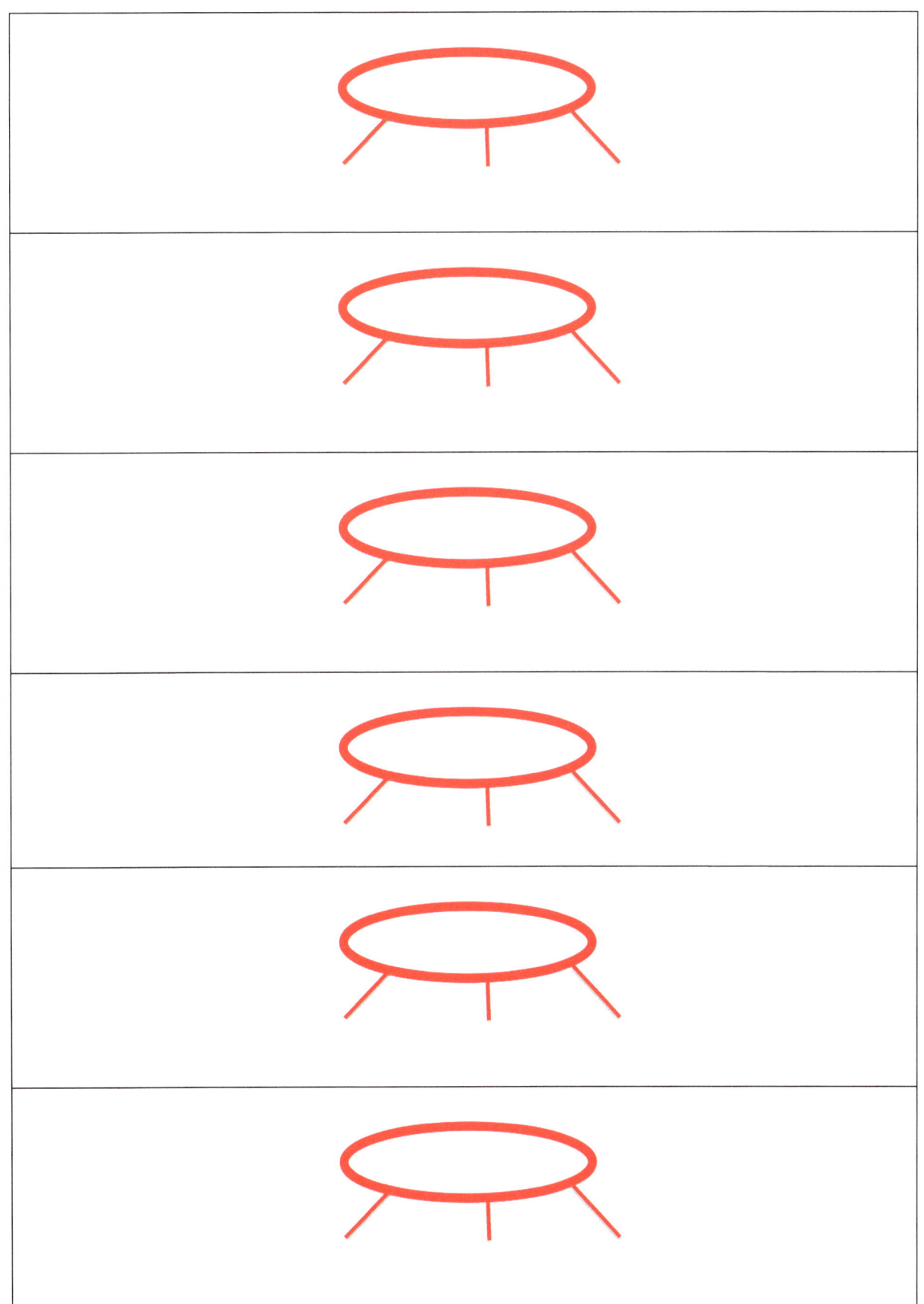

L27 Review A

Place in alphabetical order.

1. prologue
2. uniform
3. brave
4. geography
5. sadness
6. finale

L27 Review B

Unscramble the words.

1. ggaperhyo - _____
2. iurfnmo - _____
3. lopeougr - _____
4. berva - _____
5. enflia - _____
6. ssdesna - _____

L27 Test

1. _____ - an introduction or opening to a story

2. _____ - brave - courageous; fearless

3. _____ - the end

4. geography - _____

5. uniform - _____

6. sadness - _____

TRIMESTER 3 EXAM

1. grammar - _____
2. firm - _____
3. advise - _____
4. popular - _____
5. rewrite - _____
6. breathe - _____
7. conflict - _____
8. close - _____
9. except - _____
10. quiet - _____
11. selfish - _____
12. weary - _____
13. narrow - _____
14. unsure - _____
15. present - _____
16. resent - _____
17. later - _____
18. boundary - _____
19. prune - _____
20. contain - _____
21. root - _____
22. great - _____
23. cyclone - _____
24. failure - _____

25. geography - _____

26. diagram - _____

27. brave - _____

28. sadness - _____

29. barometer - _____

30. unsafe - _____

31. cheap - _____

32. prologue - _____

33. excessive - _____

34. campus - _____

35. finale - _____

36. loyalty - _____

37. action - _____

38. primitive - _____

39. powerful - _____

40. right - _____

41. careless - _____

42. waste - _____

43. dishonest - _____

44. tear - _____

45. agree - _____

46. tiny - _____

47. uniform - _____

48. ball - _____

49. transport - _____

50. night - _____

Answer Key

Lesson 1 Review A	Lesson 1 Review B
1. avoid	1. physician
2. enjoyment	2. impossible
3. fraction	3. fraction
4. impossible	4. enjoyment
5. nonsense	5. avoid
6. physician	6. nonsense
Lesson 2 Review A	**Lesson 2 Review B**
1. destroy	1. detail
2. detail	2. destroy
3. expensive	3. subzero
4. nearby	4. expensive
5. pitcher	5. pitcher
6. subzero	6. nearby
Lesson 3 Review A	**Lesson 3 Review B**
1. corporation	1. dialogue
2. dialogue	2. spectacular
3. marvelous	3. population

4. population 5. spectacular 6. startle	4. startle 5. marvelous 6. corporation
Lesson 4 Review A 1. coma 2. country 3. dangerous 4. homework 5. plot 6. research	Lesson 4 Review B 1. dangerous 2. plot 3. coma 4. research 5. country 6. homework
Lesson 5 Review A 1. brash 2. different 3. impatient 4. jog 5. pupil 6. way	Lesson 5 Review B 1. pupil 2. different 3. brash 4. impatient 5. jog 6. way
Lesson 6 Review A 1. delightful	Lesson 6 Review B 1. underground

2. exotic 3. misspell 4. smash 5. tornado 6. underground	2. misspell 3. delightful 4. tornado 5. exotic 6. smash
Lesson 7 Review A 1. drowsy 2. duck 3. equal 4. expect 5. solution 6. vigorous	Lesson 7 Review B 1. expect 2. drowsy 3. vigorous 4. solution 5. equal 6. duck
Lesson 8 Review A 1. author 2. childish 3. define 4. justice 5. sell 6. splurge	Lesson 8 Review B 1. justice 2. childish 3. sell 4. splurge 5. author 6. define
Lesson 9 Review A 1. bandit	Lesson 9 Review B 1. revise

2. common 3. monarch 4. obey 5. rage 6. revise	2. obey 3. common 4. rage 5. monarch 6. bandit
Lesson 10 Review A 1. apology 2. aquatic 3. loose 4. matriarch 5. quit 6. yard	Lesson 10 Review B 1. quit 2. loose 3. yard 4. matriarch 5. aquatic 6. apology
Lesson 11 Review A 1. break 2. desert 3. divide 4. famous 5. tire 6. whole	Lesson 11 Review B 1. tire 2. whole 3. desert 4. break 5. famous 6. divide
Lesson 12 Review A 1. disagree 2. doubt	Lesson 12 Review B 1. disagree 2. doubt 3. pair

3. humorous 4. pair 5. rash 6. subject	4. subject 5. rash 6. humorous

Lesson 13 Review A
  1. ballet
  2. dense
  3. kindness
  4. learn
  5. outstanding
  6. renew
	Lesson 13 Review B
	  1. learn
	  2. renew
	  3. ballet
	  4. kindness
	  5. outstanding
	  6. dense

Lesson 14 Review A
  1. entire
  2. peaceful
  3. remarkable
  4. slight
  5. teacher
  6. towering
	Lesson 14 Review B
	  1. remarkable
	  2. entire
	  3. towering
	  4. peaceful
	  5. teacher
	  6. slight

Lesson 15 Review A
  1. aquarium
  2. command
  3. further
  4. liberty
	Lesson 15 Review B
	  1. liberty
	  2. telephone
	  3. command
	  4. aquarium

5. steal 6. telephone	5. steal 6. further
Lesson 16 Review A 1. adopt 2. dislike 3. exquisite 4. misplace 5. precaution 6. thoughtful	**Lesson 16 Review B** 1. dislike 2. thoughtful 3. exquisite 4. adopt 5. misplace 6. precaution
Lesson 17 Review A 1. agreement 2. autograph 3. comical 4. cute 5. descent 6. desert	**Lesson 17 Review B** 1. desert 2. comical 3. agreement 4. cute 5. descent 6. autograph
Lesson 18 Review A 1. argue 2. gather 3. hear 4. meet 5. school 6. wind	**Lesson 18 Review B** 1. hear 2. argue 3. meet 4. wind 5. gather 6. school

Lesson 19 Review A	Lesson 19 Review B
1. campus 2. cyclone 3. excessive 4. great 5. loyalty 6. narrow	1. excessive 2. campus 3. narrow 4. great 5. loyalty 6. cyclone
Lesson 20 Review A	Lesson 20 Review B
1. boundary 2. close 3. diagram 4. grammar 5. later 6. powerful	1. powerful 2. boundary 3. close 4. diagram 5. later 6. grammar
Lesson 21 Review A	Lesson 21 Review B
1. conflict 2. contain 3. quiet 4. resent 5. rewrite 6. root	1. resent 2. root 3. conflict 4. rewrite 5. quiet 6. contain

Lesson 22 Review A
1. ball
2. dishonest
3. popular
4. tiny
5. unsure
6. waste

Lesson 22 Review B
1. waste
2. unsure
3. dishonest
4. popular
5. ball
6. tiny

Lesson 23 Review A
1. agree
2. careless
3. custom
4. cycle
5. transport
6. unsafe

Lesson 23 Review B
1. cycle
2. unsafe
3. custom
4. careless
5. transport
6. agree

Lesson 24 Review A
1. action
2. government
3. night
4. selfish
5. tear
6. territory

Lesson 24 Review B
1. night
2. tear
3. territory
4. selfish
5. action
6. government

Lesson 25 Review A	Lesson 25 Review B
1. breathe 2. cheap 3. failure 4. firm 5. present 6. primitive	1. present 2. breathe 3. cheap 4. failure 5. firm 6. primitive
Lesson 26 Review A	Lesson 26 Review B
1. advise 2. barometer 3. except 4. prune 5. right 6. weary	1. barometer 2. expect 3. right 4. weary 5. advise 6. prune
Lesson 27 Review A	Lesson 27 Review B
1. brave 2. finale 3. geography 4. prologue 5. sadness 6. uniform	1. geography 2. uniform 3. prologue 4. brave 5. finale 6. sadness